COPY   99

641.563 Hamrick, Becky.
H   The egg-free, milk-free, wheat-free
    cookbook / by Becky Hamrick and S.L.
    Wiesenfeld. 1st ed. New York : Harper &
    Row, c1982.
        274 p.
        ISBN 0-06-014978-7 : 16.50

    1.Cookery. 2.Food, Dietetic. I.Wiesen-
    feld, S. L. (Stephen L.)
                11671
                & 4825   082

                        81-48036
                        CIP MARC

DISCARD

The
Egg-Free
Milk-Free
Wheat-Free
Cookbook

The Egg-Free Milk-Free Wheat-Free Cookbook

BECKY HAMRICK

AND

S. L. WIESENFELD, M.D.

Illustrations by Kevin Callahan

1817

HARPER & ROW, PUBLISHERS, New York
Cambridge, Philadelphia, San Francisco,
London, Mexico City, São Paulo, Sydney

FIRST HARPER & ROW EDITION

Designed by Lydia Link

Library of Congress Cataloging in Publication Data

Hamrick, Becky.
    The egg-free, milk-free, wheat-free cookbook.

    Bibliography: p.
    Includes index.
    1. Cookery. 2. Food, Dietetic. I. Wiesenfeld, S. L.
(Stephen L.) II. Title.
TX652.H362 1982   641.5′63   81-48036
ISBN 0-06-014978-7   AACR2

---

82 83 84 85 86 10 9 8 7 6 5 4 3 2 1

TO LETA

Contents

Foreword

O ne of the great joys in life is eating. I remember well the day I told Becky Hamrick that her daughter was allergic to eggs and milk. Her astonishment and bewilderment were typical of almost all my patients with documented food allergies and their parents. "What will I feed her?" The concern is very real for a number of reasons. Eggs and milk are the foundations and often the "glue" of many foods and they help provide the basic diet of the majority of people in the Western world. With an optimism rarely seen, Mrs. Hamrick set about creating this unique cookbook which is both easy to use and allows the allergic person and his or her family to enjoy a relatively normal lifestyle.

There are great varieties of adverse reactions to foods and a variety of mechanisms. As an allergist, the most common ones I see involve the production of allergy antibodies directed specifically against parts of cow's milk, eggs and wheat. This by no means exhausts the list of potential food allergy problems, but covers at least 90% of what is seen in most allergists' offices. Many other reactions to foods are not caused specifically by allergic reactions. By this, I mean there is no allergy antibody involved. There can be specific enzyme deficiencies which do not allow the breakdown of milk or other products. There can be contaminants, noxious elements, neurologic or psychological reactions and other forms of injury of which we have no knowledge. The true prevalence of food hypersensitivity is unknown. While to me, the practicing allergist, it seems as if the world is allergic to everything, it is probably true that only 1% to 5% of infants exhibit definite allergic problems to foods which can be treated. It is also true that often individuals pass from a symptomatic to an asymptomatic stage and that hypersensitivity to foods appears to be most prevalent in childhood.

The types of symptoms which are most often seen with food allergies or hypersensitivity are extensive. With very young infants, symptoms often are related to the respiratory tract. It is common for the allergist to see a young child present with multiple ear infections, evidence of hay fever or allergic rhinitis after he or she has been seen by other physicians and been given multiple antibiotics or had tubes placed in the ear to save the hearing. Food allergies can also be present as asthma, which can be life-threatening. Other manifestations include shock, retarded growth, vomiting, stomach pain, diarrhea, malabsorption, headache, fatigue, change in activity and altered behavior and a myriad of rashes and ill-defined hives.

The diagnosis of hypersensitivity to food involves three steps. First, proof is obtained that the adverse reaction is caused by a food. This can be done by skin tests and by a blood procedure which measures allergy antibodies called RAST. Proof can also be obtained by challenging the child with the food in various ways. If foods are suspected in your child, consult your allergist. Second, the reaction must be differentiated from other causes of adverse reactions to food. Often, this can be done by history as well as examination and some simple laboratory tests. Third, the actual allergy antibody must be demonstrated in some way, either by the skin test or the RAST procedure. Other procedures have been recommended but few have withstood the test of time.

After this, your doctor will announce to you that you are the unlucky winner of an elimination diet. These gruesome mixtures of rice, lamb, tapioca and carrots can devastate the lifestyle of a family and change the emotional outlook of a child. At the same time, they can allow that child to recover some health. This cookbook allows the person suffering from food allergies to enjoy a normal life.

Perhaps two examples will show the application of the diagnostic approach to food allergies. One person came to me with a history of vomiting. Her skin test reaction to egg white was very strong and no other tests appeared to be as reactive. The RAST score confirmed that there were a great number of allergy antibodies against egg white proteins and a food challenge using a capsule with egg white so that the child could not tell what kind of food she was receiving resulted in vomiting within thirty minutes. Swelling of the larynx and tongue and a life-threatening reaction requiring her admission to the intensive care unit occurred. Another child presented with asthma and her only allergy was to cow's milk as diagnosed by history, skin tests and RAST. Ingestion of a small amount of milk provoked a severe asthma attack, which required five days of hospitalization.

It is important that the reader of this book understand that not all problems with foods are allergic. Problems with malabsorption, lack of necessary carrying proteins, deficiencies of various enzymes and other conditions may exist. Therefore, a careful examination by a physician is necessary to be sure of the diagnosis.

If you are depressed by the seeming complexity of precise diagnosis of food hypersensitivity, you will be cheered by the apparent simplicity of the treatment—avoid the food. As happened with Mrs. Hamrick, these good feelings will usually not last long, when the actual task of trying to create a diet free of offending foods is undertaken, especially when they are as elemental as eggs, milk and wheat. Hence, Mrs. Hamrick has created this indispensible tool. She has done it by creating appealing and nutritious recipes that comply with the restrictions. She, as well as I and others in my practice, have found that the entire family can enjoy these foods without any cravings for the absent ingredients. Parents are often concerned about the loss of minerals and vitamins by excluding these elements. The foods that are used contain more than enough vitamins and minerals to sustain a growing child. To be sure, a good multivitamin supplement as well as a mineral supplement can be obtained at any local supermarket. It is not necessary to resort to a health food store. For those of you with interest in health foods, you will find a wide range of new food supplements at the supermarket and more advice and information than you may ever care to absorb from your local health food store in this book.

Because of the major use of milk, eggs and wheat in diets, it is important not to incriminate too readily these foods without the evaluation I have briefly described. However, once the evidence is clear to both you and your physician, proceed with the food elimination. The results are very dramatic. Chronic ear infections subside, asthma becomes less of a problem, diarrhea ceases, recurrent life-threatening problems such as swelling in the throat stop. As Mrs. Hamrick has stated, it is important to become a compulsive label reader, and to know what to look for, as our society is not geared to those with the special needs of being intolerant to certain foods.

The natural history of food hypersensitivity in many people is the gradual loss of clinical or symptomatic reactions. If offending foods are avoided for a long enough period, usually the allergy to them is decreased or lost. Often this occurs over a period of three to five years.

There are many physicians who advocate food injections or food tablets given under the tongue. This approach has been proven time and again to be ineffective and dangerous.

You now hold in your hand one of the golden answers to food allergy—avoidance. Use it with zest and most likely, with time, the allergy will be lost. Meanwhile, food allergy's destructive process, both on the body and the life of the individual and the family, will be diminished.

We have used this cookbook in my practice for 18 months and it has been enthusiastically accepted. One day we brought in some eggfree cookies. A child who had had severe abdominal pains caused by an egg allergy picked one up. "You mean I can have a cookie and not get sick?" Yes.

STEPHEN L. WIESENFELD, M.D.
Assistant Clinical Professor
Division of Allergy and Clinical Immunology
Department of Pediatrics
Texas Tech Medical Center
Lubbock, Texas

Preface

My daughter was three years old before we discovered that she had allergies. Before that, she was always sick, most of the time with pneumonia. The pediatrician gave her antibiotics and temporarily made her well, but within two to four weeks she was sick again. I asked him about her going to see an allergist and he told me that she would "outgrow it." I finally took it upon myself to get an appointment with Dr. Wiesenfeld. I knew that it wasn't normal for anyone to be sick as much as she had been.

We discovered that Leta's problems were due to allergies. I was to eliminate eggs, milk and wheat in any form from her diet.

I panicked. Leta enjoyed a glass of milk with every meal, as well as eggs for breakfast, and I couldn't think of many things that she ate that didn't contain wheat. She knew and loved the taste of all the foods that contained one or all of these ingredients. Fortunately, she wasn't as allergic to wheat, so my main concern was eggs and milk.

In the beginning, I cheated a little and would give her foods that had milk and eggs in them or a piece of cheese every once in a while. I thought that just a little wouldn't hurt. I was wrong. She got sick and Dr. Wiesenfeld asked me if I was sticking to her diet, and I told him no. That convinced me that I had to eliminate eggs and milk in any form. It worked, and Leta's health improved within weeks.

I went to the library and checked out all of the books that I could find on food allergies and recipes that would be helpful. I tried these recipes and they just didn't have the same taste as the food that they were trying to replace. I decided to try things on my own. I started experimenting with different recipes and incorporating some of the ideas that I had found in the books. I had a lot of failures, but I learned from them and the next attempt was a success. My main objective was to cook egg-free, milk-free and some wheat-free foods and make them taste the same as the foods that they were replacing. I also wanted the recipes and their ingredients to be simple. If recipes are simple, they will be used more and won't scare anyone away.

I have realized that with a little imagination and some knowledge just about any recipe can be changed to fit your allowed diet. There are replacements for nearly all of the foods that you are allergic to. In the section called "Food Allergy Cooking Hints," I have listed some of the replacements that I have found. I have listed a lot of different flours and their equivalence to wheat flour so you can replace wheat flour with these flours in your own recipe and any of the recipes in this book that are not wheat-free. I've also discussed replacements for eggs and milk. Please read the "Cooking Hints" section. By using some of the ideas you will be able to take your favorite recipes and make them egg-free, milk-free and wheat-free.

There are a lot of prepared foods in the grocery store that are egg-free, milk-free and wheat-free. In the "Cooking Hints" section, I have listed all of the names used to list the use of eggs, milk and wheat in a product. Learn these names and check the ingredients on the package. READ THE LABELS. You'll be surprised at all of the goodies that are free of all three ingredients, or at least eggs and milk.

The response to the diet has been overwhelming. Not only people with food allergies, but heart patients also have found the book extremely helpful. The comments I most often hear are that the foods taste great, they're easy to prepare and the entire family can enjoy them. Just knowing that this book is helping people makes all of the effort worthwhile.

I'm writing this book because it will help a lot of people discover that a food allergy doesn't have to be so limiting. Try these recipes and let your whole family enjoy them.

BECKY HAMRICK

Food Allergy Cooking Hints

Being on an allergy diet means that you have to omit allergy-producing foods from your diet. To accomplish this, there are two things you must do. First, you must learn to read labels and familiarize yourself with the ingredients in your favorite products, and second, you must know how to prepare more dishes without the allergenic items. It is important to understand that cooking in conformity with allergic needs does not necessarily mean that unusual ingredients must be used. This book will give you an interesting selection of recipes that have perfectly "normal" ingredients.

MILK

Label readers should know that the following terms mean milk in some form:

lactose
caseinate or sodium caseinate or casein
lactalbumen
lactoglobulin
curds
whey

Further, the "nondairy" products are not always milk-free. Some, such as the following, contain caseinate (milk protein):

Cool Whip
Richning
Coffee-Mate
Preen

1

The following are acceptable because they do not contain either milk or caseinate:

Coffee Rich
Lucerne Frozen Non-Dairy Creamer
Rich's Rich Whip

There are numerous substitutes that you can use in place of milk. Soybean milk is good for the younger child who still drinks milk in quantity. It can even be whipped in the blender to resemble a milk-shake. Instant powdered soybean milk which can be mixed like dried milk is available in most health-food stores. All soybean milks have a stronger flavor than milk, but can be used for drinking or in cooking and baking and have the nutritional value comparable to milk. Soy-bean milk in whatever form is greatly helped by chilling. It can also be poured over dry cereals or hot cereals. Fruit juices or stewed fruits also make an interesting addition to cereals in place of milk.

When it comes to cooking, water can generally be used just as regular milk would be. Also coconut milk, fresh or canned coconut juice can be used for baking or in beverages.

"Nondairy" liquid creamer may be used in almost any recipe except custards, puddings and delicate cakes. Use full strength for coffee and rich cream sauce. Dilute two parts creamer to one part water for regular cream sauce, hot cereals, or making cream pies and dessert sauces. Keep some on hand, already diluted with equal parts of water, for general use such as poured over dry cereals. Diluted this way, nondairy liquid creamer has the same number of calories as whole milk, but not the nutritional value.

Kosher products such as kosher margarine, bread and processed meats labeled "parve" or "pareve" do not contain milk, nor do most diet margarines (Diet and Light Parkay Margarine). Here again, you must read the labels.

EGGS

If the following items appear among the listed ingredients, egg pro-tein is contained in the product somewhere:

albumin
vitellin or ovovitellin

livetin
yolk
powdered or dried egg
globulin
ovomucoid
ovomucin

Eggs not only bind a recipe together, but they also add volume. Usually you can substitute one teaspoon of egg-free baking powder (Clabber Girl) for each egg called for in a recipe. This works well in recipes that have peanut butter or another ingredient that contains oil.

Here is a home recipe that can replace one egg in a recipe for baking:

EGG EQUIVALENT

1½ tablespoons oil
1½ tablespoons water
1 teaspoon baking powder (eggfree)

Beat all of the ingredients together and add to the recipe just as you would one egg. If the recipe calls for more than one egg, double the amount of oil, water and baking powder.

WHEAT

If the following items are among the listed ingredients, the product contains wheat:

wheat flour (or just plain flour)
graham flour
gluten flour
enriched flour
hydrolized vegetable protein or the initials hvp
monosodium glutamate or MSG

REPLACEMENTS FOR WHEAT FLOUR

For one cup of wheat flour, you may substitute any one of the following:

½ cup arrowroot

½ cup barley—particularly good for cakes, but can be used in almost all baked goods; its products retain moistness for several days.

1 cup corn flour—smooth flour which should be blended with other flours for baking.

¾ cup cornmeal (coarse)—gives a coarse texture, but is very tasty in various breads.

1 scant cup cornmeal (fine)

½ cup cornstarch—do not use waxy type for baking; light in texture, must be handled carefully or it will lump.

¾ cup oats—use in combination with other flours.

1⅓ to 1½ cups oats (ground rolled)—use in combination with other flours.

¾ cup potato meal—grainy, used in small amounts; can lighten the texture of bread.

⅝ cup potato starch—gives light, fluffy texture; used alone in some cakes and in combination with other flours in breads and rolls.

¾ to ⅞ cup rice flour—do not use waxy type for baking; a very light flour, it is usually combined with other flours.

¾ to 1 cup rye flour—produces a much heavier texture than wheat. Rye bread must be kneaded thoroughly and raised carefully.

1 cup rye meal

¾ cup soybean flour—has an oily texture and unusual flavor and should be used with other flours.

COMBINATIONS EQUAL TO 1 CUP WHEAT FLOUR:

½ cup potato flour and ½ cup rye flour

⅓ cup potato flour and ⅔ cup rye flour

½ cup potato-starch flour and ½ cup soy flour

⅝ cup rice flour and ⅓ cup rye flour

1 cup soy flour and ¼ cup potato-starch flour

The best bet is to make a mixture of flours, using two or more grains, for baking. Mix, store in a container and use in almost any recipe that calls for wheat flour. The following mixture yields a good all-purpose flour (except for making light bread):

1 cup cornstarch
2 cups rice flour
2 cups soy flour
3 cups potato-starch flour

This flour should be baked at lower temperatures than wheat flour and for a longer period of time.

A combination of flours is often more palatable than a single flour. Combinations should be sifted together three times to ensure good mixing and then thoroughly mixed with other dry ingredients. Baking time is usually longer with flours other than wheat by per-haps ten to twenty minutes, especially when milk and eggs are omit-ted from the recipe. A lower baking temperature is also better.

Do not be concerned if batters appear thinner than usual wheat flour batters.

Refrigerating dough mixture for thirty minutes makes the dough easier to handle and improves the appearance of the final product.

Cakes made from other than wheat flours are likely to be more dry. Frosting plus storing in a closed container will help. Fruits, chocolate chips and nuts added to cakes will improve the texture.

Muffins and biscuits made from nonwheat flours have better texture when made small.

THICKENING AGENTS OTHER THAN WHEAT:

Arrowroot:	1 tablespoon	=	2½ tablespoons wheat flour
Barley flour:	1 tablespoon	=	1 tablespoon wheat flour
Cornstarch:	½ tablespoon	=	1 tablespoon wheat flour
Oatmeal:	1 tablespoon	=	1 tablespoon wheat flour
Potato starch:	½ tablespoon	=	1 tablespoon wheat flour
Rice flour:	½ tablespoon	=	1 tablespoon wheat flour
Sago:	½ tablespoon	=	1 tablespoon wheat flour
Tapioca:	½ tablespoon	=	1 tablespoon wheat flour

Breakfast Ideas

PANCAKES AND WAFFLES

APPLESAUCE PANCAKES

1½ cups rice flour
2 tablespoons potato-starch flour
3 tablespoons cornstarch
½ teaspoon salt
1½ teaspoons baking powder (egg-free)
1 teaspoon lemon juice
1 cup sweetened applesauce
3 tablespoons melted milk-free margarine
1 cup water
2 tablespoons oil, 4 tablespoons water, and 2 teaspoons baking powder (egg-free), beaten together

In a medium bowl, stir together rice flour, potato-starch flour, cornstarch, salt and 1½ teaspoons baking powder. Add lemon juice, applesauce, melted margarine, 1 cup water, and beaten together oil, water, and baking powder. Mix well. Drop by ¼ cupfuls onto heated griddle; lightly spread each pancake with back of spoon into a circle about 4 inches in diameter. Cook until rim of each is full of broken bubbles and underside is brown. Turn and brown other side.
Makes 16.

OATMEAL PANCAKES

¾ cup quick oats
¼ teaspoon baking soda
1½ cups water
½ cup ground oats (grind in a blender)
1 tablespoon sugar
1 teaspoon baking powder (egg-free)
½ teaspoon salt
3 tablespoons oil, 2 tablespoons water and 1 teaspoon baking powder (egg-free), beaten together

Combine oats, baking soda and 1½ cups water; let stand for 5 minutes. Combine ground oats, sugar, 1 teaspoon baking powder and salt. Add to this beaten together oil, water and baking powder and beat well.

Pour ¼ cup batter for each pancake onto a hot greased griddle. Bake to a golden brown, turning once.

Makes 10.

RICE-POTATO PANCAKES

½ cup rice flour
⅓ cup potato flour
¼ teaspoon salt
4 teaspoons sugar
½ teaspoon baking powder (egg-free)
⅓ to ½ cup water
1½ tablespoons oil, 1½ tablespoons water and 1 teaspoon baking powder (egg-free), beaten together

Sift dry ingredients together. Beat in ⅓ to ½ cup water. Beat in the mixture of oil, water and baking powder. Cook on a hot greased griddle, using about ¼ cup batter for each pancake. Turn once.

HONEY AND GRANOLA HOTCAKES

1 cup flour
1 tablespoon baking powder (egg-free)
½ teaspoon salt
1¼ cups water
2 tablespoons oil
2 tablespoons honey
½ cup crushed granola

In mixing bowl stir together flour, baking powder and salt. In small bowl combine water, oil and the honey; add all at once to dry ingredients, beating until blended. For each hotcake, pour about ¼ cup batter onto hot, lightly greased griddle. Sprinkle each hotcake with 1 tablespoon granola. Bake until rim of hotcake is full of broken bubbles and underside is brown; turn and brown other side. Serve with Honey Syrup (see below).
Makes 8.

HONEY SYRUP
⅓ cup honey
¼ cup maple-flavored syrup

Heat together the honey and maple-flavored syrup.
Makes ⅔ cup.

WAFFLES OR PANCAKES

2 cups flour
4 teaspoons baking powder (egg-free)
½ teaspoon salt
2 tablespoons sugar
2 cups water (more may be used to acquire desired thickness)
3 tablespoons oil
¼ teaspoon vanilla extract
¼ teaspoon butter flavoring

Sift dry ingredients together. Add the remaining ingredients and beat. Bake in a hot waffle iron or on a hot griddle.

Note: 1 cup of blueberries, strawberries or any other berry, fruit or nut may be added for variety.

MUFFINS

BANANA NUT MUFFINS

½ cup vegetable oil
1 cup sugar
3 tablespoons oil, 3 tablespoons water and 2 teaspoons baking powder (egg-free), beaten together
2 bananas, mashed
2 cups flour
1 teaspoon baking soda
¼ cup chopped nuts

Preheat oven to 400 degrees. Mix the above in the order given. Beat until just blended. Fill greased muffin cups ⅔ full and bake for about 20 to 30 minutes in preheated oven.

ORANGE BRAN MUFFINS

　1½ cups all-bran cereal
　　1 cup orange juice
　　¼ cup water
　1½ tablespoons oil, 1½ tablespoons water and 1 teaspoon bak-
　　　ing powder (egg-free), beaten together
　　⅓ cup oil
　1½ cups flour
　　3 teaspoons baking powder (egg-free)
　　1 teaspoon salt
　　½ cup brown sugar, firmly packed
　　1 tablespoon grated orange rind

Preheat oven to 400 degrees. Combine bran cereal, orange juice and ¼ cup water in a bowl. Add the oil, water and baking powder mixture, then the ⅓ cup oil; mix well. Combine flour, baking powder, salt, sugar and grated orange rind. Stir into first mixture until dampened. Spoon into paper-lined muffin cups. Bake for 25 to 30 minutes.
Makes 12.

APPLE MUFFINS

　1½ tablespoons oil, 1½ tablespoons water and 1 teaspoon bak-
　　　ing powder (egg-free), beaten together.
　　1 cup apple juice
　　⅓ cup oil
　1¾ cups sifted flour
　　4 teaspoons baking powder (egg-free)
　　¾ teaspoon salt
　　¼ cup sugar
　　¼ teaspoon nutmeg
　　¾ cup shredded apple
　　1 teaspoon grated lemon rind

Preheat oven to 400 degrees. Into the oil, water and baking powder mixture, stir in apple juice and ⅓ cup oil. Sift dry ingredients into liquid mixture. Stir just enough to dampen the flour mixture. Batter should be lumpy; do not overmix. Add apple and lemon rind; blend lightly. Fill paper-lined muffin cups ⅔ full. Bake for 25 to 30 minutes.

Makes 12.

BRAN MUFFINS

> ¼ cup solid vegetable shortening
> ¼ cup brown sugar, firmly packed
> ⅔ cup apple juice or any other juice
> 1 tablespoon oil, 2 tablespoons water and 1 teaspoon baking powder (egg-free), beaten together
> ¼ cup molasses
> 1 cup flour
> 1 cup bran
> 1 tablespoon baking powder (egg-free)
> ¼ teaspoon salt
> ½ to 1 cup raisins (optional)

Preheat oven to 400 degrees. Beat together shortening and sugar until light and fluffy. Blend in juice, the oil, water and baking powder mixture, and the molasses. Combine remaining dry ingredients and add to mixture; mix just until dry ingredients are moistened. Add raisins. Fill 12 muffin cups lined with paper cups ⅔ full. Bake for about 15 minutes.

Makes 12.

RYE AND RICE MUFFINS

⅔ cup unsifted rye flour
⅓ cup rice flour
2 teaspoons baking powder (egg-free)
¼ teaspoon salt
4 teaspoons sugar
½ cup water
3 tablespoons oil

Preheat oven to 400 degrees. Grease 6 muffin pans. Stir together the rye flour, rice flour, baking powder, salt and sugar. In a medium bowl stir the water and the oil into the flour mixture until just mixed, but still lumpy. Divide batter among muffin cups. Bake 30 to 35 minutes, or until muffins come away from edges of pan.
Makes 6.

RYE MUFFINS

1 cup unsifted rye flour
2 teaspoons baking powder (egg-free)
2 tablespoons sugar
¼ teaspoon salt
½ cup water
2 tablespoons oil

Preheat oven to 400 degrees. Grease 6 muffin pans. Sift together the rye flour, baking powder, sugar and salt. Add the water and oil and stir just until mixed, but still lumpy. Divide the batter among the muffin cups. Bake 30 to 35 minutes, or until muffins come away from the edges of the pan.
Makes 6.

PINEAPPLE MUFFINS
Make Rye Muffins but reduce sugar to 1 tablespoon; stir 2 tablespoons drained canned crushed pineapple into dry ingredients; substitute ½ cup pineapple juice for water.

BACON MUFFINS

Make Rye Muffins but mix 1 cooked and crumbled bacon strip with dry ingredients; reduce oil to 1 tablespoon.

CINNAMON RAISIN MUFFINS

Make Rye Muffins but stir ½ teaspoon cinnamon and ½ cup raisins into dry ingredients.

NUT MUFFINS

Make Rye Muffins but add ½ cup chopped nuts to dry ingredients.

DATE MUFFINS

Make Rye Muffins but add ¼ cup cut-up pitted dates to dry ingredients.

PEANUT BUTTER MUFFINS

Make Rye Muffins but cut ¼ cup peanut butter into dry ingredients until consistency of cornmeal; omit oil.

OAT MUFFINS

1 cup sifted oat flour
⅛ teaspoon salt
3½ teaspoons baking powder (egg-free)
1½ teaspoons sugar
¼ cup cold water
2 tablespoons melted milk-free margarine

Preheat oven to 425 degrees. Sift dry ingredients into a bowl. Add cold water and mix until smooth. Stir in the margarine. Pour into muffin cups that have been greased. Bake for 25 minutes.

Makes 6 to 8 muffins.

CORN MUFFINS

1 cup cornmeal
¾ cup rice flour
5 teaspoons baking powder (egg-free)
½ teaspoon salt
¼ cup sugar
1 tablespoon oil
¼ cup melted milk-free margarine
1 cup water

Preheat oven to 425 degrees. Grease 12 muffin pans. In a medium bowl, stir together the cornmeal, rice flour, baking powder, salt and sugar. Add 1 tablespoon oil, margarine and the cup of water to the dry ingredients; stir until smooth. Divide batter among muffin cups (about ¼ cup each). Bake 25 minutes or until muffins pull away from the sides of the cups. Turn muffins out.
Makes 12.

BREAKFAST BREADS AND ROLLS

MAPLE NUT ROLLS

        1½ cups lukewarm water
        1 tablespoon dry yeast
        ¼ cup maple syrup or honey
    3½ to 4 cups flour
        1 teaspoon salt
        ¼ cup oil
        1 cup raisins
        1½ cups flour
        ½ cup maple syrup
        1 cup chopped walnuts

In a large bowl, combine water and yeast. Stir until it dissolves and add ¼ cup syrup or honey.

Stir in the flour, beating with rounding strokes. Beat about 50 times. Cover the bowl with a cloth and set in a warm place to rise for 1 hour.

Fold in the salt and oil until thoroughly mixed.

Add the raisins and the 1½ cups flour. Knead on a floured board until smooth and elastic. Place the dough in an oiled bowl, oil the top and cover. Set in a warm place to rise for 40 minutes. Punch down. Roll out ¾ inch thick. Cut in 2-inch circles. Put maple syrup and nuts into 2 small bowls and dip each circle first into the syrup and then into the nuts. Place them nut side down on a greased cookie sheet about ¼ inch apart. Cover with a cloth and let rise for 20 minutes. Bake 25 minutes at 350 degrees. When done, turn over to serve.

CINNAMON ROLLS ⊘🍞

½ recipe Hot Rolls (page 153)
1 tablespoon milk-free margarine
2 teaspoons cinnamon
2 tablespoons sugar
½ cup raisins or pecans (optional)
Confectioners' Sugar Frosting (page 212)

Roll dough out until it is about ⅛ inch thick. Dot with milk-free margarine and sprinkle all over with sugar and cinnamon. (Raisins or pecans may be added if desired.) Begin rolling from one side until it is a big roll. Cut into 1-inch-thick rounds, place in a greased pan and let rise until doubled. Bake at 450 degrees 10 to 15 minutes, or until golden brown. Ice the rolls with frosting when cool.

QUICK CINNAMON ROLLS ⊘🍞

1 can egg-free, milk-free prepared biscuits (see note below)
¼ cup milk-free margarine
½ teaspoon cinnamon
¼ cup granulated sugar
¼ cup raisins (optional)
¼ cup sugar

Flatten biscuits into rectangle shape. Dot with margarine; sprinkle with mixture of cinnamon and sugar, reserving some for muffin tins. Add raisins. Roll up, beginning with the wide shape, into an oblong roll. Cut in 1- to 1½-inch slices. Place in muffin tins which contain remainder of margarine and brown sugar. Bake at 425 degrees for 10 to 12 minutes.
Makes 6 servings.

Note: Pillsbury or Hungry Jack Buttermilk Biscuits, Artificially Flavored, are two brands of biscuits that are egg-free and milk-free.

QUICK PULL-APART BREAD

2 cans milk-free, egg-free prepared biscuits (see note above)
½ teaspoon cinnamon
½ cup granulated sugar
⅓ to ½ cup milk-free margarine
½ cup brown sugar
½ teaspoon cinnamon

Cut the biscuits into quarters. Roll each quarter into a ball and roll into the mixture of ½ teaspoon cinnamon and ½ cup sugar. Melt the margarine and add ½ cup brown sugar and ½ teaspoon cinnamon. Grease a bundt pan and spread with 2 or 3 tablespoons of the brown-sugar mixture. Roll the biscuits in the remaining mixture and pile them into the bundt pan. Pour balance of brown-sugar mixture over all. Bake at 350 degrees for 30 to 35 minutes. Cool for 10 minutes.

SPICED RAISIN LOAVES

2 cups brown sugar, firmly packed
2 cups water
1 15-ounce package raisins
2 tablespoons milk-free margarine
1 teaspoon salt
1 teaspoon cinnamon
¼ teaspoon ground cloves
3 cups flour
1 teaspoon baking soda

In a 3-quart saucepan, combine the first seven ingredients. Over medium heat, heat to boiling. Reduce heat to low and simmer for 5 minutes. Let cool, then refrigerate the raisin mixture until thickened and chilled, about 2½ hours, stirring occasionally. Preheat oven to 325 degrees. Grease and flour two 8½ × 4½-inch loaf pans. In a large bowl, mix the flour, baking soda, and chilled raisin mixture until flour is thoroughly moistened. Divide batter between loaf pans. Bake for

1 hour and 10 minutes or until a toothpick inserted in centers comes out clean. Cool in pans for 10 minutes; remove from pans and cool completely. To store, cover with plastic wrap and refrigerate.

Makes 2 loaves.

EASY BISCUIT CINNAMON ROLLS ⊖ ⊕

½ cup milk-free margarine
¾ cup sugar
2 tablespoons cinnamon (more or less to taste)
2 cans egg-free, milk-free prepared biscuits (see note on page 18)

Preheat oven to 350 degrees. Melt margarine in a baking pan. Mix together in a small bowl ¾ cup sugar and 2 tablespoons cinnamon. Break each biscuit apart. Dip into melted margarine, then into the cinnamon mixture. Place in the pan with the margarine. Continue this until both cans of biscuits are used. The pan should be completely full. Place in oven and bake until biscuits are done (about 15 minutes). Remove from oven and spread with orange glaze while they are still hot. Serve hot or cold.

ORANGE GLAZE ⊖ ⊕ ⊕
1½ cups powdered sugar
Juice from 1 orange or 3 tablespoons of orange juice

Combine the above ingredients. If the icing is still thick, gradually add a little water to make it stir easily.

DOUGHNUTS

DOUGHNUTS

1 can egg-free, milk-free prepared biscuits (see note on page 18)
Hot oil
Powdered sugar

Separate each biscuit, flatten into a circle and cut a hole in the middle. In a heavy pan, heat about 4 inches of oil to 360 degrees and fry the doughnuts a few at a time until golden brown on both sides, turning once. Drain on paper towels. Roll them in powdered sugar while they are still warm and after they have cooled. (The centers can also be fried.)

JELLY-FILLED DOUGHNUTS

Use same ingredients as in Doughnuts recipe, above. Tear each biscuit in half and fry in hot oil. Brown and drain. Let cool and fill the center with desired jelly or chocolate icing or anything else that you enjoy. Then roll in powdered sugar.

Appetizers

THE GUACAMOLE RING   ⊖♯♣

2 envelopes unflavored gelatin
1 cup water
2 tablespoons lemon juice
1 teaspoon salt
½ teaspoon garlic powder
½ teaspoon hot pepper sauce
4 medium avocados, peeled, seeded, mashed
¼ cup finely chopped onion

In small saucepan, sprinkle unflavored gelatin over cold water, let stand 1 minute. Stir over low heat until gelatin is completely dissolved, about 5 minutes. Stir in lemon juice, salt, garlic powder and hot pepper sauce. In large bowl, using wire whip or beater, combine gelatin mixture with avocados; stir in onion. Pour into 5-cup ring mold or individual molds; chill until firm. Serve as an appetizer salad or as a spread for crackers.

Makes about 5 cups.

GUACAMOLE DIP   ⊖♯♣

1 avocado
½ cup diced fresh tomato
1 tablespoon minced onion
½ teaspoon garlic salt
1 tablespoon lemon juice or vinegar
½ cup canned Mexican green chili sauce (Salsa verde)
Salt and pepper to taste

Mash avocado; add remaining ingredients. Serve as a dip or as individual servings on lettuce.

PINEAPPLE SHRIMP ⊖⊕✳

1 14-ounce can chunk pineapple in syrup
2 tablespoons soy sauce
2 tablespoons lemon juice
1 tablespoon salad oil
1 teaspoon dry mustard
24 large shrimp, cooked, shelled and deveined
Macadamia nuts or peanuts, finely chopped
Flaked coconut

Drain pineapple. Blend together ¼ cup pineapple syrup, soy sauce, lemon juice, oil, and mustard. Pour over shrimp; cover and let stand ½ hour. Meanwhile, soak 8 bamboo skewers in water.

Alternate 3 shrimp and 4 pineapple chunks on each skewer. Brush on remaining marinade. Place on rack or in shallow pan. Broil 2 to 3 inches from heat, turning and basting until hot and lightly browned, 3 to 5 minutes. Sprinkle with nuts and coconut.

CHICKEN LIVER ROLLUPS ⊖⊕✳

¼ cup soy sauce
1 tablespoon Worcestershire sauce
2 tablespoons water
¼ teaspoon garlic powder
6 chicken livers, quartered
12 water chestnuts, cut in half
6 bacon slices, quartered

Mix soy sauce, Worcestershire sauce, water and garlic powder in a pint jar; add livers and water chestnuts. Marinate at least 2 hours or overnight. Turn or shake jar occasionally to soak chestnuts and livers thoroughly. Remove from liquid. Wrap a piece of chicken liver and a slice of water chestnut with a piece of bacon. Secure with a toothpick. Broil for 5 to 7 minutes, or until bacon is crisp.

COCKTAIL WIENERS

¾ cup prepared mustard
1 cup currant jelly
8 to 10 frankfurters

Mix mustard and jelly in chafing dish or double boiler. Diagonally slice frankfurters into bite-size pieces. Add to sauce and heat thoroughly. Serve with toothpicks.

SPICY FRANKFURTER APPETIZERS

1 jar of Safeway brand spaghetti sauce (or any other sauce that is egg-free and milk-free)
1 to 2 pounds frankfurters, cut in 1-inch pieces

Combine the above ingredients and refrigerate until serving time. Heat frankfurters in sauce. Serve in casserole over candle warmer at table. Or heat and serve from chafing dish. Provide toothpicks.

SAUSAGE CRESCENTS ⟨symbol⟩

   1 can refrigerated crescent dinner rolls (be sure they are egg-
     free and milk-free)
  16 brown n' serve sausages

Cut crescent triangles in half, making two small triangles. Place a sausage on each small triangle and roll up. Bake at 375 degrees on an ungreased baking sheet for 10 to 13 minutes, or until golden brown.

BROILED CHICKEN LIVERS ⟨symbol⟩

  1 pound sliced lean bacon
  1 pound frozen chicken livers

Cut slices of bacon in half. Roll ½ slice bacon around each chicken liver. Secure with toothpick. Broil until bacon is cooked on one side. Turn and broil on other side 6 to 8 minutes or until done. Serve at once.

BACON 'N' ONION APPETIZER ⟨symbol⟩

  ½ pound bacon
  ⅓ cup brown sugar
  1 small jar cocktail onions, drained

Cut bacon slices into thirds. Dip in brown sugar. Wrap bacon pieces, sugared side in, around cocktail onions. Secure with tooth-picks. Broil about 2 minutes on each side. May be served hot.

SHRIMP COCKTAIL ⊖❤❦

1 pound medium shrimp
Remoulade Sauce (page 65)
Lettuce leaves for garnish

Cook, shell and devein the shrimp. Chill, pour sauce over shrimp, and serve over lettuce leaves as a first course on a salad plate or in a cocktail glass, or serve as an appetizer in a bowl accompanied by shrimp stuck on toothpicks inserted in a snack holder.

CAPONATA ⊖❤❦

2 medium eggplants, cubed
1 tablespoon salt
3 tablespoons oil
1 8-ounce can tomato sauce
1 large onion, finely chopped
2 celery stalks, finely chopped
1 clove garlic, finely chopped
10 green olives, quartered
1 teaspoon vinegar
Sugar and salt to taste

Sprinkle eggplant cubes with salt and allow to drain in a colander for about 30 minutes. Squeeze out lightly. Cook in hot oil until tender; add tomato sauce. Sauté onion, celery, garlic and olives in a small amount of oil; add vinegar. Mix all ingredients together with sugar and salt and cook until flavors are blended. Cool. Serve on crackers or with meats.

Soups
Salads
Dressings
Sauces

SOUPS

GUMBO

  2 tablespoons milk-free margarine
  ⅓ cup chopped onion
  ⅓ cup chopped green pepper
  ⅓ cup chopped celery
  1 small clove garlic, finely chopped
  ½ cup diced okra
1½ cups canned tomatoes
  1 cup chicken broth
  ⅔ teaspoon salt
  ⅓ teaspoon sugar
Few grains pepper
Small pinch thyme
Small piece bay leaf
  1 cup uncooked shrimp, peeled and deveined
  1 cup oysters

Melt margarine in a large skillet. Add onion, green pepper, celery and garlic. Cook until vegetables are lightly browned. Add okra, tomatoes, broth and the seasonings. Cover and simmer for 30 minutes. Add shrimp. Cook 5 minutes. Add oysters and continue cooking for 1 minute, or until edges of oysters curl slightly.

Makes 4 servings.

Note: Another cup of shrimp may be used instead of oysters.

CREAM-OF-MUSHROOM SOUP SUBSTITUTE

¼ cup minced onion
2 tablespoons minced celery
1 clove garlic, minced
3 tablespoons milk-free margarine
½ pound fresh mushrooms, chopped
¼ cup flour
1 cup chicken or beef broth (or 1 bouillon cube dissolved in
    1 cup hot water)
½ teaspoon basil (optional)
¾ teaspoon salt
Pinch of sugar
1½ cups nondairy creamer

Sauté onion, celery and garlic in milk-free margarine until soft. Add mushrooms and brown lightly. Sprinkle flour over, stirring constantly over low heat until all flour is blended in. Gradually add broth, seasonings and creamer. Bring to boil slowly and simmer for 2 minutes, stirring constantly. Makes about 2½ cups, or the equivalent of 2 cans of commercial cream of mushroom soup.

VEGETABLE SOUP

5 tablespoons milk-free margarine
½ cup carrot, cut small
½ cup celery, cut small
½ cup turnip, cut small
½ cup potato, cut small
1 quart water
Salt and pepper
½ tablespoon finely cut parsley

Melt 4 tablespoons margarine in a large saucepan and add carrots, celery and turnips. Cook and stir 10 minutes. Add potatoes, cover and cook 2 minutes.

Add the water and boil uncovered until vegetables are tender. Season with salt and pepper and rest of margarine, sprinkle with parsley, and serve hot.

HEARTY SALADS

HOT POTATO SALAD

10 cups diced cooked potatoes
10 slices bacon (½ pound)
1½ cups chopped onion
⅔ cup bacon drippings
5 tablespoons flour
3 tablespoons sugar
2 to 3 teaspoons salt
¾ teaspoon celery seed
⅛ teaspoon pepper
1½ cups water
¾ cup vinegar
¼ cup chopped pimento (2 ounces)
Parsley

Place potatoes in a 2½-quart casserole. Fry bacon until crisp. Drain and save drippings. Cook onion in ⅔ cup bacon drippings for about 5 minutes or until clear. Remove from heat.

Mix together flour, sugar, salt, celery seed and pepper; blend into drippings mixture over low heat. Gradually pour in the water and vinegar, stirring until mixture boils. Pour over potatoes. Add bacon, broken into small pieces, and pimento. Mix lightly.

Cover casserole and place in a 325-degree oven for 30 minutes, or until bubbly and heated thoroughly. Garnish with parsley and serve.

Makes 8 to 10 servings.

TASTY SALAD 🖊️🎗️🎋

1½ cups sugar
½ cup vinegar
½ cup salad oil
⅓ cup water
1 No. 303 can small peas, drained
1 can green string beans, drained
1 bunch celery, finely cut
1 green pepper, finely cut
1 jar pimento, drained and chopped
1 small onion, grated
½ teaspoon salt

Mix sugar, vinegar, oil and water together. Combine remaining ingredients. Pour liquid mixture over vegetables. Cover and refrigerate.

SEAFOOD MOLDED SALAD 🖊️🎗️🎋

1 package lemon gelatin
1 cup boiling water
½ cup chili sauce
2 tablespoons grated horseradish
1 teaspoon Worcestershire sauce
2 drops Tabasco sauce
½ cup finely cut celery
1 can shrimp, cleaned
1 can crab meat, flaked

Dissolve gelatin in boiling water. In a 1-cup measuring cup combine chili sauce, horseradish, Worcestershire and Tabasco sauces. Fill remainder of cup with cold water and add to gelatin. Chill. When slightly congealed add celery, shrimp and crab meat. Chill.

MOLDED SHRIMP SALAD

1½ packages lemon gelatin
2 cups V-8 juice
2 tablespoons vinegar
1 cup cooked shrimp, deveined
2 tablespoons chopped onion
2 tablespoons chopped celery
2 tablespoons chopped green pepper

Add lemon gelatin to V-8 juice and simmer for 2 to 3 minutes. Add vinegar, stir and pour into bowl. Chill until slightly thickened. Add shrimp, onion, celery and green pepper. Chill.

MOLDED TUNA SALAD

1 cup English peas, drained
1 package lemon gelatin
1 cup boiling water
2 tablespoons lemon juice
½ cup salad dressing (one that is tolerated)
1 cup white-meat tuna
¼ cup diced pimento
½ cup sliced stuffed olives
⅓ cup chopped pecans
⅔ cup diced celery

Drain peas and reserve liquid. Dissolve gelatin in boiling water; add ½ cup liquid from peas and lemon juice. Refrigerate until slightly set. Fold in salad dressing; add flaked tuna and remaining ingredients. Pour into mold; chill until firm.

BRIGHT SALAD

1 package lemon gelatin
1 cup hot water
1 teaspoon salt
¼ teaspoon garlic salt
Dash of pepper
1 tablespoon vinegar
½ cup cold water
1 cup cooked shrimp, cut into ½-inch pieces
1 avocado, diced

Dissolve gelatin in hot water. Add seasonings, vinegar and cold water. Pour into 8-inch square pan. Chill until slightly thickened. Add shrimp and avocado pieces arranged so they will be in small cubes when cut. Chill until firm. Cut into 1-inch squares.

SALAD BASE

1½ cups grapefruit sections
1 cup diced fresh tomato
½ cup sliced ripe olives
¼ cup chopped green onions
3 quarts salad greens

Combine ingredients and toss lightly. Arrange shrimp and avocado squares on top. Serve with favorite salad dressing.

JELL-O SALAD

> 1 large package orange gelatin
> 2½ cups boiling water
> 2 apples, peeled and chopped
> 2 stalks celery, chopped
> 1 cup whole cranberries
> 1 can (16 ounces) crushed pineapple
> 1 tablespoon lemon juice

Prepare Jell-o by following the package directions. When it has started to set, fold in the remaining ingredients.

SUNNY SALAD

> 2 tablespoons lemon juice
> 2 tablespoons orange juice
> 2 teaspoons sugar
> ½ teaspoon salt
> 1 cup grated cabbage
> 1 cup grated carrots
> 1 cup chopped apples

Combine lemon juice, orange juice, sugar and salt. Pour over cabbage, carrots and apples; toss.

WEST INDIES CRAB-MEAT SALAD

1 pound fresh crab meat
1 medium onion, finely chopped
Salt and pepper
½ cup salad oil
½ cup vinegar
½ cup ice water

Pick over crab meat to remove bits of shell and cartilage. Place half of the chopped onion in bottom of bowl. Arrange crab meat on top of onion. Spread remaining onion over crab. Salt and pepper to taste. Pour oil, then vinegar and lastly ice water over crab mixture. Cover and refrigerate from 2 to 12 hours. Toss lightly just before serving.

HAM AND RICE SALAD

1⅓ cups raw rice
1½ tablespoons dry mustard
2 tablespoons cold water
1½ tablespoons sugar
1½ tablespoons wine vinegar
¼ cup salad oil
½ cup chopped green pepper
1 cup diced cooked ham
½ cup cooked peas
Parsley, chopped
Salad greens

Prepare rice as directed on package. Mix mustard, water, sugar and vinegar; gradually beat in oil. Stir lightly into warm rice. Cool; add green pepper, ham and peas. Sprinkle with parsley and serve with greens.

SHRIMP SALAD ⬚

1 cup chopped cooked shrimp
1 cup diced celery
1 teaspoon lemon juice
1 teaspoon finely chopped onion
Salt and paprika to taste
Low Calorie French Dressing (page 60) or Mayonnaise (page 61)
Lettuce leaves for garnish

Mix first 5 ingredients lightly. Chill. Just before serving, drain and toss together with desired dressing. Serve on crisp lettuce.

VEGETABLE SALAD ⬚

1 small onion, chopped
3 stalks celery, chopped
1 green pepper, chopped
1 can English peas, drained
1 can cut or French green beans, drained
1 small jar pimentos, drained and chopped
1 teaspoon salt

DRESSING
¾ cup sugar
1 cup vinegar
½ cup corn oil
½ teaspoon paprika

Combine vegetables; sprinkle with salt. Refrigerate, covered, overnight. Next morning drain, mix all dressing ingredients, and mix vegetables with dressing. This salad will keep in the refrigerator for several days.

PINEAPPLE AND CARROT SALAD

1 3-ounce package lemon gelatin
1 cup boiling water
1½ cups pineapple juice
1 28-ounce can crushed pineapple, drained
1 cup grated carrots
1 tablespoon vinegar

Dissolve gelatin in boiling water. Add pineapple juice. Cool. Add remaining ingredients; stir. Pour into 1½ quart mold. Chill.

THREE-BEAN SALAD

¼ cup chopped onion
1 can green beans
1 can yellow wax beans
1 can red kidney beans

Drain all vegetables; rinse the kidney beans. Place in a bowl and add Sweet and Sour Salad Dressing (below). Marinate several hours. Serve salad well chilled.

SWEET AND SOUR SALAD DRESSING
½ cup salad oil
½ cup vinegar
¾ cup sugar
½ teaspoon salt
½ teaspoon pepper

Mix all ingredients.

GOLDEN GATE BEAN SALAD 🔲

2 packages frozen Italian green beans
1 cup cauliflowerets
½ cup sliced celery
2 tablespoons chopped pimento
French dressing
Lettuce leaves
4 slices bacon, fried and crumbled

Cook beans according to package directions; drain. Add cauliflowerets, celery and pimento. Toss lightly with French dressing. Chill. Serve on lettuce leaf with crumbled bacon on top.

MIXED VEGETABLE SALAD 🔲

2 packages frozen mixed vegetables
½ cup sliced scallions
½ cup finely sliced raw cauliflower
½ cup stuffed olives, sliced; or ¼ cup diced pimento
Garlic Vinaigrette Dressing (see below)

Cook mixed vegetables according to package directions. Drain and chill. Combine all ingredients and marinate in dressing for 1 hour before serving.

GARLIC VINAIGRETTE DRESSING
⅓ cup salad oil
3 tablespoons wine vinegar
1 clove garlic, crushed
1½ teaspoons salt
⅛ teaspoon pepper

Combine all ingredients; mix well.

TOSSED APPLE-SPINACH SALAD

1 pound fresh spinach
1½ cups cored, diced apples
1 small red onion, thinly sliced
2 tablespoons lemon juice
1 tablespoon salad oil
¼ teaspoon salt
¼ teaspoon Worcestershire sauce
1 teaspoon sugar

Remove stems and large ribs from spinach; tear up larger leaves. Wash in several changes of water. Place in a large saucepan with water still clinging to the leaves, cover and steam 1 to 2 minutes or until slightly wilted. Use no additional water. Drain off any liquid from spinach. Place in salad bowl with diced, unpared apples and onion rings. Combine remaining ingredients. Pour over salad and toss lightly.

SIDE-DISH SALADS

EVERYDAY SLAW

4 cups shredded cabbage
½ cup sliced green onions
1 cup sliced celery
⅓ cup sugar
⅓ cup vinegar
⅔ cup salad oil
½ teaspoon salt

Combine cabbage, onions and celery. Mix sugar, vinegar, salad oil, and salt. Blend well. Pour desired amount of dressing over cabbage mixture.

CABBAGE SKILLET SALAD ⌀⊖♦

4 slices bacon
¼ cup vinegar
1 tablespoon brown sugar
1 teaspoon salt
1 tablespoon finely chopped onion
4 cups shredded cabbage
½ cup chopped parsley

Cook bacon until crisp. Remove from pan and crumble. Add vinegar, sugar, salt and onion to bacon drippings. Add crumbled bacon. Heat thoroughly. Remove from heat. Toss cabbage and parsley in hot dressing.

CABBAGE SALAD ⌀⊖♦

1 medium onion
2 cups shredded green cabbage
2 cups shredded red cabbage
2 small apples, sliced
½ cup salad oil
¼ cup vinegar
1 teaspoon celery seed
1 teaspoon salt

Slice half of onion into rings; chop remaining half. Combine chilled red and green cabbage with chopped onion in a large bowl. Arrange row of chilled apple slices and onion rings on top. Combine salad oil, vinegar, celery seed and salt. Just before serving pour over salad and toss.

SWEET AND SOUR COLE SLAW

1 medium head cabbage, shredded
1 medium onion, chopped
1 medium green pepper, chopped
1 tablespoon salt
1 cup vinegar
1½ cups sugar
1 teaspoon celery seed
½ teaspoon mustard seed

Combine vegetables and salt in a large pan. Cover with boiling water, cover pan and let stand for 1 hour. Drain well and return to pan. Heat vinegar, sugar and spices until sugar dissolves. Pour over vegetables; mix well. Store in a glass container in refrigerator. Let flavors blend for a day before serving. Keeps for several weeks in refrigerator.

COLE SLAW

1 medium head cabbage, shredded
1 green pepper, chopped
1 medium onion, chopped
2 tablespoons sugar

Mix together the above.
Bring to boil the following ingredients and pour over the cabbage mixture:

1 teaspoon celery seed
1 cup vinegar
½ cup salad oil
2 tablespoons sugar
1 teaspoon salt

This should set at least 12 hours in refrigerator. It will keep for several days.

FRUIT SALADS

HAWAIIAN FRUIT SALAD

1 cup cubed fresh pineapple, or canned pineapple chunks
1 cup white seedless grapes
1 cup cubed cantaloupe or papaya
1 cup shredded coconut or angel-flake coconut
½ cup nondairy whipped topping

Combine pineapple, grapes, cantaloupe and coconut. Toss lightly with the topping.

BLUEBERRY FRUIT SALAD

2½ cups (1 No. 2 can) blueberries
2 packages raspberry gelatin
2¼ cups hot water
Blueberry juice
1 cup nondairy whipped topping

Drain berries and reserve juice. Mix 1 package of gelatin with 1½ cups hot water. Add ½ cup blueberry juice. Cool until slightly set. Pour into 1-quart mold. Chill. Mix remaining gelatin with ¾ cup hot water and ½ cup blueberry juice. Cool. Add topping and blueberries. Pour on top of chilled mixture. Chill several hours or overnight.

CARROT-LIME SURPRISE SALAD

1 6-ounce package lime gelatin
2 cups boiling water
1½ cups cold water
2 cups grated carrot
1 cup crushed pineapple
1 cup miniature marshmallows
½ cup chopped walnuts

Dissolve gelatin in boiling water. Add cold water. Chill until mixture is partially congealed. Whip with electric mixer or rotary beater until light and fluffy. Add carrots, pineapple, marshmallows and walnuts. Mix thoroughly. Chill until firm.

SUNGLOW RAISIN SALAD

⅔ cup light or dark raisins
1 package lemon gelatin
1¼ cups hot water
2 tablespoons lemon juice
1 cup crushed pineapple, undrained
¼ teaspoon salt
1¼ cups grated carrots

Rinse raisins; cover with water and boil for 5 minutes. Cool and drain. Dissolve gelatin in hot water. Blend in lemon juice, pineapple and salt. When slightly thickened, fold in raisins and carrots. Turn into individual molds. Chill until firm.

APRICOT SALAD

2 envelopes unflavored gelatin
½ cup cold water
2 cans apricots, drained (reserve juice)
18 marshmallows
Juice of 1 lemon
½ teaspoon salt

Dissolve gelatin in water. Bring apricot juice to boil; add marshmallows. Remove from heat and stir until marshmallows are melted. Add lemon juice, salt and gelatin to hot juice; cool. Add apricots. Chill until firm.

APRICOT GELATIN

1 package apricot gelatin
3 ripe bananas, thinly sliced
1 small can crushed pineapple, drained
Nondairy whipped topping

Dissolve gelatin according to package directions; cool. Fold in bananas combined with pineapple. Chill until firm. Top with nondairy whipped topping.

EASY CHRISTMAS SALAD θ♯♣

    1 package lime gelatin
    1 cup hot water
    1 cup crushed pineapple, drained
Juice from pineapple plus water to make 1 cup
    1 tablespoon lemon juice
    2 cups miniature marshmallows
    1 small bottle Maraschino cherries, drained
    ½ cup walnuts

Dissolve gelatin in hot water. Add juices. Chill until nearly firm. Fold in pineapple, marshmallows, cherries and nuts. Chill until firm. For a festive touch: Barely cover bottom of mold with diluted gelatin; arrange cherries and marshmallows, chill until firm. Add mixture to this.

MOLDED WALDORF SALAD θ♯♣

    1 envelope unflavored gelatin
    ⅓ cup sugar
    ½ teaspoon salt
    1½ cups water
    ¼ cup vinegar or lemon juice
    2 cups diced tart apples
    ½ cup diced celery
    ¼ cup chopped pecans

Mix gelatin, sugar and salt thoroughly in a small saucepan. Add ½ cup of the water. Stir over low heat, until gelatin is dissolved. Remove from heat; stir in remaining water, vinegar or lemon juice. Chill mixture until thickened. Fold in apples, celery and nuts. Chill until firm.

CRANBERRY DELIGHT

1 pound cranberries, coarsely ground
2 oranges, peeled (reserve rind) and chopped
2 cups sugar
3 or 4 pineapple slices, chopped
3 or 4 apples, chopped

Grind orange rind into cranberries; add sugar and mix well. Mix in orange and pineapple pieces. Add apples just before serving. Serve in a hollowed orange half if desired.

GRAPE-CANTALOUPE SALAD

1 can chunk pineapple
½ cantaloupe
1½ cups seedless grapes
1 banana, sliced
1 tablespoon cornstarch
1 cup miniature marshmallows

Drain pineapple and reserve juice. Cut fruit into bite-size pieces. Heat pineapple juice; add cornstarch and cook 2 or 3 minutes, or until clear. Cool. Pour dressing over combined fruits and marshmallows.

APPLE SALAD

4 apples, chopped
¼ cup diced celery
¼ cup chopped dates
¼ cup chopped nuts
3 tablespoons sugar
Maraschino cherries

Combine apples, celery, dates and nuts. Sprinkle with sugar; toss. Chill. Garnish with cherries. Salad keeps 4 to 5 hours.

FRESH FRUIT SALAD

4 medium bananas, sliced
8 oranges, chopped
1 pound grapes, seeded and halved
¼ cup chopped nuts
1½ cups miniature marshmallows
1 cup nondairy whipped topping
Maraschino cherries

Mix all the fruit together. Add nuts and marshmallows. Chill. Just before serving, add the whipped topping and mix. Top with maraschino cherries.

BING CHERRY SALAD

1 No. 2 can Bing cherries, drained
1 to 2½ cups crushed pineapple, drained (optional)
2 packages cherry, lime or blackberry gelatin
2 Coca-Colas
2 cups fruit juice
1 cup chopped nuts (optional)
Nondairy whipped topping (optional)

Heat juices drained from cherries and pineapple. Pour over gelatin; stir well. Cool. Add Coca-Cola. Chill until partly congealed. Add fruit juice and nuts. Chill until firm. Garnish with nondairy whipped topping, if desired.

GRAPEFRUIT SALAD

2 envelopes unflavored gelatin
½ cup cold water
1 No. 2 can grapefruit, drained
1 No. 2 can cherries, drained and pitted
1 No. 2 can sliced pineapple, drained and cubed
Juice of 1 lemon
Pinch of salt
1 cup slivered almonds

Soften gelatin in cold water. Combine grapefruit, cherry, pineapple juices; bring to boil. Remove from heat; add softened gelatin and lemon juice. Cool. Add remaining ingredients. Pour into molds and chill until firm.

FRENCH PINEAPPLE SALAD ⊘✝✦

1 large pineapple
Sugar
1 large orange, sectioned and peeled
2 peaches, sliced
1 banana, slant sliced
1 apple, sliced
1 pint strawberries, hulled and sweetened
1 cup pecan halves

Cut pineapple in half lengthwise, remove fruit and cut into cubes. Dust cubes with sugar. Combine with remaining ingredients. Chill for 30 minutes. Lightly pile fruit into pineapple shells.

JELLIED AMBROSIA SALAD ⊘✝✦

1 envelope plain gelatin
¼ cup cold water
¼ cup boiling water
2 tablespoons sugar
1¼ cups orange juice
2 tablespoons lemon juice
3 medium oranges, peeled and sectioned
1 large banana, peeled and sliced
¼ cup grated or shredded coconut

Soften gelatin in cold water. Dissolve in boiling water. Add sugar; stir over low heat until completely dissolved. Add orange and lemon juice. Cool until thickened. Add fruit and coconut to orange-juice mixture. Pour into molds; chill until firm. Garnish with orange sections, a sprinkle of coconut and sprigs of fresh mint.

FROZEN FRUIT CUP

1 cup canned fruit cocktail or diced fresh fruit
½ cup seedless grapes
½ cup watermelon balls
1 small bottle ginger ale, chilled
Mint leaves

Mix fruits, place in ice-cube tray. Pour ginger ale over fruit and freeze 1½ to 2 hours or until mixture is a mush. Serve in small sherbet glasses and garnish with mint leaves.

CANTALOUPE SALAD COCKTAIL

1 cantaloupe
2 peaches, sliced
1 cup cubed honeydew melon
1 cup halved seeded grapes
¼ cup French fruit dressing (See below)

Cut cantaloupe lengthwise into 8 wedges; chill. Combine peaches, honeydew melon and grapes with dressing. Chill 1 hour. For each serving arrange 2 cantaloupe wedges to form oval or circle and fill centers with fruit mixture.

FRENCH FRUIT DRESSING
⅓ cup sugar
1 teaspoon salt
1 teaspoon paprika
¼ cup orange juice
2½ tablespoons lemon juice
1 tablespoon vinegar
1 cup salad oil
1 teaspoon grated onion

Combine ingredients in a bottle or jar; cover and shake thoroughly.
Makes 1¾ cups

FRESH PEAR SALAD AND DRESSING ⊘∰

DRESSING
>   2 tablespoons flour
>   ½ cup sugar
>   2 tablespoons lemon juice

Mix all ingredients; cook over low heat until flour is cooked and clear. Be careful not to scorch. Cool.

>   2 cups diced or sliced fresh pears
>   1 cup diced celery
>   ⅓ cup pecans
>   Salad greens
>   Maraschino cherries (optional)

Mix the pears and celery in the dressing; add nuts. Serve on salad greens. Garnish with cherries if desired.

Note: A combination of ¼ cup honey and 2 tablespoons lemon juice may be substituted for the cooked dressing if desired.

CHERRY SALAD ⊘∰✳

>   1 can cherry pie filling
>   1 small can crushed pineapple, drained
>   1 cup chopped pecans
>   1 cup miniature marshmallows
>   1 cup sugar
>   3 bananas, sliced

Mix first 5 ingredients and let stand overnight in the refrigerator. Stir in bananas just before serving.

EASY FRUIT SALAD ⚘🏵✽

1 can instant peach pie filling
1 can fruit cocktail, drained
1 can pineapple tidbits, drained
1 can Mandarin oranges, drained
1 cup chopped apples, (optional)
1 can grapes, drained
1 cup miniature marshmallows
1 banana, sliced
1 cup chopped nuts

Combine pie filling, fruit cocktail, pineapple, oranges, apples and grapes. Add marshmallows, banana and nuts. Refrigerate several hours before serving.

MELON COOLER ⚘🏵✽

1 honeydew melon (about 5 pounds)
1 package (3 ounces) gelatin dessert (lime, orange or strawberry)
1 cup boiling water
2 cups crushed ice cubes
1 banana, sliced

Cut melon in half lengthwise; scoop out seeds and drain well. Dissolve gelatin in boiling water. Add ice cubes and stir until gelatin begins to thicken, about 3 minutes. Remove any unmelted ice. Stir in banana. Place melon halves in small bowls; spoon in gelatin mixture. (Chill any excess fruited gelatin in a dessert dish.) Chill until firm. Cut in wedges.
Makes 6 servings.

GEL-FRUIT SALAD

1 envelope unflavored gelatin
2 tablespoons sugar
¼ cup water
Juice of 1 lemon
1½ cups ginger ale
1 apple, diced
½ cup diced fresh strawberries
1 banana, diced
1 11-ounce can Mandarin orange segments, drained and diced

Mix gelatin and sugar in a saucepan. Add water and lemon juice. Stir constantly over low heat until gelatin and sugar dissolve. Remove from heat. Add ginger ale. Chill until mixture is partially firm. Fold in fruits. Chill until firm.

CHERRY SALAD MOLD

2 packages orange gelatin
1 cup hot water
Cherry syrup plus enough water to make 1 cup liquid, heated
1 7-ounce bottle ginger ale
Orange syrup plus enough water to make 1 cup liquid
1 1-pound can dark, sweet cherries or 1 pint frozen sweet cherries, drained and pitted (reserve juice)
1 11-ounce can Mandarin orange sections, drained (reserve juice)
⅓ cup nuts, broken

Dissolve gelatin in hot water and cherry liquid, Add ginger ale and orange liquid; chill until mixture is syrupy. Pour ¾ cup of the thick mixture into a ring mold. When mixture starts to congeal, alternately place cherries and orange sections on top. Cover with remaining gelatin, nuts, cherries and orange sections combined. Chill until firm.

MOLDED MANDARIN SALAD

2 packages orange gelatin
2 cups hot water
1 12-ounce can frozen orange juice
2 small cans Mandarin oranges, undrained

Dissolve gelatin in hot water. Add orange juice. Let set until partially congealed. Add oranges, mix well; chill until firm.

CINNAMON-APPLESAUCE SALAD

1 tablespoon red cinnamon candies
1 cup hot water
1 package cherry gelatin
2 cups applesauce, sweetened
½ cup chopped celery
½ cup chopped nuts

Dissolve candy in hot water; pour over gelatin. Add applesauce and chill until partially set. Fold in celery and nuts. Chill until firm.

SUNSET SALAD

2 packages strawberry gelatin
2 cups hot water
1 cup cold water
1 can cranberry sauce, mashed
4 bananas, diced
½ cup chopped pecans

Dissolve gelatin in hot water, add cold water. Chill until partially thickened. Fold cranberry sauce, bananas and nuts into gelatin. Pour into molds that have been rinsed in cold water. Chill until firm.

CRANBERRY HOLIDAY SALAD ⌂⌂⌂

1 package lemon or raspberry gelatin
1 cup hot water
½ cup cold water
2 cups uncooked cranberries, chopped
1 to 3 thin-skinned oranges, chopped
1 to 3 red apples, chopped
1½ cups sugar
½ to 1 cup nuts
1 cup chopped celery (optional)

Dissolve gelatin in hot water; add cold water. Chill until partially set. Combine fruits, sugar, nuts and celery. Fold into gelatin. Chill until firm.

STRAWBERRY DELIGHT ⌂⌂⌂

1 package lemon gelatin
1 package strawberry gelatin
2 cups boiling water
2 packages frozen strawberries
1 cup crushed pineapple
2 bananas, diced
½ to 1 cup nuts (optional)

Thoroughly dissolve gelatins in boiling water. Add strawberries; stir until berries separate and thaw. Mixture will begin to congeal. Add pineapple, bananas and nuts. Pour mixture into a mold. Chill until firm.

TROPICAL SALAD ✐✿❀

 1 3-ounce package strawberry gelatin
 1 3-ounce package orange gelatin
 2 cups hot water
 3 oranges, sectioned
 1 8½-ounce can sliced pineapple, undrained and cut in wedges
 1 10-ounce package frozen strawberries

Dissolve gelatins in hot water. Add oranges, pineapple wedges and strawberries. Chill until firm.

SALAD DRESSINGS

FRENCH DRESSING ✐✿❀

 1 cup vegetable oil
 ½ cup sugar
 ⅓ cup ketchup
 ¼ cup vinegar
 1 teaspoon salt
 1 teaspoon paprika
 1 tablespoon onion juice or 1 small onion, grated

Combine all ingredients; mix with beater. Dressing will be fairly thick and will not separate too much if thoroughly mixed.

LOW-CALORIE FRENCH DRESSING ☒

1 clove garlic, sliced
¼ cup vinegar
¾ teaspoon salt
⅛ teaspoon pepper
¼ teaspoon paprika
2 teaspoons sugar
½ cup tomato juice
2 tablespoons water
2 tablespoons vegetable oil

Add garlic to vinegar; let stand for 20 minutes. Strain. Combine salt, pepper, paprika and sugar in a jar. Add tomato juice, water, vinegar and oil. Cover and shake vigorously. Store in refrigerator. Shake again before using.

DRESSING FOR SPINACH SALAD ☒

½ cup oil
2 tablespoons vinegar
2 tablespoons sugar
1 teaspoon grated onion
¼ teaspoon dry mustard
½ teaspoon salt

Combine all ingredients and shake well to mix. Keep in refrigerator.

MAYONNAISE I 🖉🌂🌸

  1½ tablespoons potato flour (or other flour)
   ¼ teaspoon dry mustard
   ½ teaspoon salt
   2 teaspoon sugar
   ¼ cup cold water
   ¾ cup boiling water
   2 tablespoons lemon juice
   1 tablespoon white vinegar
   ½ cup salad oil
Salt and pepper to taste

Mix dry ingredients in saucepan, stir in cold water and mix well. Add hot water and cook just until mixture is clear. Cool to lukewarm, then gradually add remaining ingredients, beating constantly.

MAYONNAISE II 🖉🌂🌸

   ¼ teaspoon salt
   ¼ teaspoon sugar
   ¼ teaspoon paprika
   ¼ teaspoon celery salt
   ½ teaspoon dry mustard
Dash of cayenne pepper
   3 tablespoons nondairy liquid creamer
   ½ cup salad oil
   4 teaspoons lemon juice or vinegar

Mix dry ingredients and creamer together. Beat in salad oil gradually. Stir in lemon juice. Refrigerate in covered jar.
Makes ¾ cup.

HONEY–CELERY SEED DRESSING

¾ cup salad oil
2 tablespoons cider vinegar
2 tablespoons fresh lemon juice
1 teaspoon salt
½ teaspoon paprika
½ cup honey
¾ teaspoon celery seed
½ teaspoon grated lemon rind

Combine all ingredients in blender or jar. Blend or shake until thoroughly mixed. Chill. Shake before using. Make dressing at least 1 day before using for improved flavor.
Makes 1½ cups.

OIL DRESSING

2 teaspoons salt
2 teaspoons paprika
2 teaspoons dry mustard
2 teaspoons celery seed
1 cup sugar
½ cup vinegar
2 tablespoons grated onion
2 cups warm salad oil

Mix all ingredients together, adding oil last. Warm the dressing in a pan set in hot water. Beat until thick. Refrigerate.

THOUSAND ISLAND DRESSING

1 cup mayonnaise (your own diet type)
4 tablespoons chili sauce
1 tablespoon grated onion
3 tablespoons ketchup
1 teaspoon vinegar or pickle juice
2 tablespoons chopped green pepper
1 tablespoon chopped red pepper
1 teaspoon paprika

Mix ingredients well and chill.

MEAT GRAVY I

Pan fat from roast meat or poultry
¼ cup flour
2 cups boiling water
¼ teaspoon salt, or to taste

Pour off all but ¼ cup of the pan fat. Put pan on stove on low heat and add flour. Stir and blend until flour is brown, about 2 minutes. Add the boiling water slowly, stirring all the time. Bring mixture to the simmering point and add salt. Cook 5 minutes.

MEAT GRAVY II

3 tablespoons pan fat from roast
3 tablespoons rice flour
2 cups cold water
Salt and pepper to taste

Pour fat from roasting pan, being careful to leave the brown meat juices in pan. Measure 3 tablespoons of meat fat into roasting pan, then stir in 3 tablespoons rice flour. Slowly add 2 cups cold water and cook over low heat, stirring constantly, until gravy boils and thickens. Season to taste with salt and pepper.

OR: Combine 4½ teaspoons cornstarch gradually with 2 cups cold water, stir into 3 tablespoons fat in pan and cook, stirring constantly, until thickened. Season to taste.

WHITE SAUCE

2 tablespoons milk-free margarine
¼ cup flour
¼ teaspoon salt
Dash of pepper
½ cup water
1 cup liquid nondairy creamer

Melt milk-free margarine in saucepan; blend in flour, salt, pepper and water. Add creamer. Cook and stir until thickened and sauce comes to a boil.

Note: To make a thinner sauce, reduce flour to 2 tablespoons.

TARTAR SAUCE

½ cup mayonnaise (to fit your allowed diet)
1 teaspoon chopped parsley
2 teaspoons sweet pickle relish
2 teaspoons capers
1 teaspoon minced onion

Combine all ingredients; chill to blend flavors.

REMOULADE SAUCE

¼ cup vinegar
1½ tablespoons prepared mustard
Horseradish to taste
½ teaspoon salt
¼ teaspoon cayenne pepper
1½ teaspoons paprika
1 tablespoon catsup
½ clove garlic, mashed to paste
½ cup salad oil
¼ cup finely minced green onions and tops
¼ cup finely chopped celery

Combine vinegar, mustard, horseradish, salt, pepper, paprika, catsup and garlic. Mix well. Add salad oil; beat vigorously. Add green onions and celery. Chill.

Main Dishes

BEEF

SPECIAL STUFFED MEAT LOAF

¼ pound ground beef
1 potato, grated
1¼ teaspoons salt
¼ teaspoon pepper
¼ teaspoon sage
2 tablespoons tomato juice
1 cup canned whole-kernel corn
1 onion, thinly sliced
1 cup drained and chopped whole tomatoes
Salt and pepper to taste

Combine beef, potato, salt, pepper, sage and tomato juice. Spread half of mixture in greased loaf pan. Add layers of corn, onion and tomatoes. Season with salt and pepper. Cover with remaining meat mixture. Bake at 350 degrees for 1 hour.
Makes 6 servings.

EASY MEAT LOAF

1½ pounds ground round steak
1 package dried onion soup
1 can chicken and rice soup

Combine meat, dried onion soup and undiluted chicken and rice soup. Mix well and form into a meat loaf. Place in a greased loaf pan and bake 1½ hours at 350 degrees.

POT ROAST AND VEGETABLES

1 pot roast
Small amount of oil
1 cup water
1 small onion, sliced
4 carrots, sliced
2 potatoes, sliced

Season pot roast to taste. Pour just enough oil into a large deep pot to cover the bottom of it. Brown the roast on all sides. Pour 1 cup of water in, cover, and let it cook slowly for 2 to 3 hours. After 1½ hours, put in the vegetables and cover; continue simmering until meat is tender.

SWISS STEAK I

1 pound round steak
Potato meal
Salt and pepper
3 tablespoons oil
½ cup chopped onion
½ cup chopped celery
½ cup water
1 small can peeled tomatoes

Dredge the meat well with potato meal which has been seasoned with salt and pepper. Brown meat in oil. Add remaining ingredients. Cover and bake at 325 degrees for 1½ hours, or until very tender.

SWISS STEAK II ⊖♋

1 pound round steak, cut into pieces
Cornflakes, crushed
Flour
2 tablespoons milk-free margarine
1 teaspoon parsley
Pinch of savory

Dredge pieces of round steak with cornflakes and pound with edge of heavy plate or mallet, adding as much flour as steak will hold. Melt the milk-free margarine in a skillet and sear steak. Add the parsley and a pinch of savory. Cover and bake at 275 degrees for 2 hours, or cook on top of stove on lowest heat; watch to avoid burning. Add water as needed.

BEEF 'N' PEPPER STEAK ⊖♋♦

1 pound beef tenderloin, sliced ¼ inch thick
2 tablespoons salad oil
1 medium onion, sliced
1 large green pepper, cut in 1-inch cubes
1 clove garlic, minced
1 cup bouillon
1 tablespoon soy sauce
1½ tablespoons cornstarch
¼ cup water
2 small tomatoes, cut into sections

Brown beef in oil. Push to one side of pan. Add onion, pepper, garlic; cook 5 minutes or until vegetables are softened. Add bouillon, soy sauce, and cornstarch dissolved in the water. Cover; simmer 10 minutes or until meat and vegetables are tender. Add tomatoes. Heat through. Serve with rice.

Makes 4 servings.

ROUND STEAK CASSEROLE ⊖⊕✦

  1½ pounds round steak, cut in ½-inch pieces
  3 tablespoons milk-free margarine
  1 medium onion, chopped
  5 small potatoes, sliced
  3 carrots, sliced
Seasonings to taste
  2 cups beef bouillon

Brown steak in margarine; remove from pan. Sauté onion in drippings until lightly browned. Layer half of meat, onion, potatoes and carrots in a shallow baking dish. Season to taste. Repeat layers. Pour bouillon over all. Cover and bake at 300 degrees for 2 hours. Add more bouillon if necessary.

Makes 4 to 6 servings.

SWEET AND SOUR BEEF ⊖⊕✦

  1 8-ounce can pineapple chunks
  1 cup cubed cooked beef (leftover roast)
  ½ green pepper, cut in thin strips
  ½ onion, cut in thin rings
  3 tablespoons oil
  ⅔ cup brown sugar, firmly packed
  ⅔ cup water
  ⅓ cup tomato ketchup
  ¼ cup vinegar
  2 tablespoons cornstarch
Hot cooked rice

Drain pineapple, reserving juice, and set aside. In a large skillet, sauté beef, green pepper and onion in oil. Combine brown sugar, water, tomato ketchup, vinegar, cornstarch and pineapple juice in saucepan. Bring to a boil, stirring constantly until thickened. Pour over beef mixture. Gently stir in pineapple chunks; simmer 15 minutes. Serve over rice.

Makes 2 servings.

STUFFED CABBAGE CASSEROLE

12 large cabbage leaves
¾ pound ground beef
¾ pound ground pork
¾ cup cooked rice
1 teaspoon salt
¼ teaspoon pepper
¼ teaspoon powdered garlic
¼ to ½ cup water
1 can tomato soup
¼ cup water
1 small can tomato sauce
4 strips uncooked bacon

Cook cabbage leaves in boiling water a few minutes to soften; drain and remove core end. Combine beef, pork, rice, salt, pepper, garlic and ¼ to ½ cup cold water. Mix thoroughly and divide into 12 sections. Place each section on cabbage leaf; roll, beginning at wide end. Place each roll into a casserole dish. Mix soup, ¼ cup water and tomato sauce. Pour over cabbage rolls. Place strips of bacon on top. Bake uncovered at 350 degrees for 45 minutes to 1 hour.

Makes 6 servings.

AMERICAN SUKIYAKI

2 onions, peeled and diced
1 stalk celery, diced
1 bunch carrots, peeled and diced
1 can bamboo shoots, diced
¼ cup milk-free margarine
1½ pounds beef sirloin, cut in slivers
1 cup beef broth, heated
4 teaspoons soy sauce

Sauté vegetables in milk-free margarine for 7 minutes. Add beef; sauté 7 minutes longer. Add hot beef broth and soy sauce. Serve over rice.

Makes 4 servings.

ITALIAN SPAGHETTI SAUCE

1 pound ground beef
3 small cans tomato sauce
1 can tomatoes
1 teaspoon garlic salt
½ teaspoon oregano
⅛ teaspoon pepper
¼ teaspoon salt
1 bay leaf

Brown ground beef; add remaining ingredients. Simmer uncovered about 1 hour. Serve over spaghetti.
Makes 6 to 8 servings.

PORCUPINE MEATBALLS

1 pound ground beef
½ cup uncooked rice
1 teaspoon salt
⅛ teaspoon pepper
1 small onion, sliced
½ green pepper, sliced
1 tablespoon oil
2½ cups tomato juice
Dash of nutmeg
Salt and pepper to taste

Combine ground beef, rice, salt and pepper. Form into balls about 1½ inches in diameter. Place in baking dish. In a skillet, brown onion and green pepper in oil. Add tomato juice, nutmeg and salt and pepper to taste. Pour over meatballs. Cover baking dish. Bake at 350 degrees for about 1 hour or until rice is very tender.
Makes 8 meatballs.

BEEF, LAMB, OR VEAL RAGOUT e♯♦

2 pounds beef, lamb, or veal cut for stew
2 celery stalks, cut in ½-inch pieces
1 medium onion, cut in 8 pieces
2 medium carrots, split lengthwise and cut in 1-inch pieces
1 16-ounce can tomatoes
⅓ cup minute tapioca
2½ teaspoons salt
½ teaspoon pepper
1 bay leaf

Combine all ingredients in Dutch oven or 2-quart casserole. Cover and bake at 300 degrees for 3 hours. Remove bay leaf. Serve with boiled potatoes.

Makes about 7 cups or 7 servings.

BEEF AND RICE WITH CELERY e♯

⅔ cup uncooked rice
1½ cups diced celery
3 tablespoons chopped onion
2 tablespoons melted milk-free margarine
1 pound ground beef chuck
1 teaspoon salt
⅛ teaspoon pepper
1 tablespoon milk-free margarine
1 can tomato soup, condensed
¼ cup water

Cook rice according to the directions on the package. Place in a greased 2-quart casserole. Brown celery and onion lightly in the 2 tablespoons milk-free margarine. Place on top of rice. Season beef with salt and pepper and brown in 1 tablespoon margarine. Place on top of celery-onion mixture. Combine soup and water. Pour over all. Bake uncovered at 375 degrees for 35 minutes.

MEAT-STUFFED PEPPERS

    2 large or 4 small green peppers
    1 pound ground beef
    1 tablespoon minced onion
    ½ teaspoon salt
    ⅛ teaspoon pepper
    1 cup cooked rice
    ½ cup ketchup

Cut the green peppers in half lengthwise, remove seeds and parboil in salted water for 5 minutes. Drain. Combine the beef, onion, salt, pepper and rice and spoon the mixture into the green pepper halves. Place in a shallow pan and bake uncovered at 350 degrees for 35 minutes. Top with ketchup and bake 5 minutes longer.

HAMBURGER GOOP

    1 cup chopped onion
    1 cup chopped green pepper
    1 cup chopped celery
2 to 3 tablespoons vegetable oil
    1½ pounds ground beef
    1 small can tomato soup or 1 small can tomato sauce
    2 tablespoons barbecue sauce
    1 teaspoon chili powder
    2 teaspoons salt
    ½ teaspoon pepper
Hot dog or hamburger buns

Cook onion, green pepper and celery in oil until limp. Add ground beef and brown. Pour tomato soup over meat; stir in barbecue sauce, chili powder, salt and pepper. Cover and simmer 30 minutes. Spoon over hot dog or hamburger buns.
Makes 8 to 10 servings.

VEGETABLE-MEAT CASSEROLE

1 pound ground beef
1 onion, chopped
1 cup diced carrots
2 cups canned tomatoes, undrained
1 cup canned whole-kernel corn, drained
½ cup uncooked rice
1 green pepper, chopped
2 cups boiling water
2 teaspoons salt
Pepper to taste

Brown meat; add rest of ingredients. Stir. Put into casserole and cover. Cook in 350-degree oven for 2 hours.
Makes 6 servings.

HAMBURGER-BISCUIT BAKE

3 tablespoons chopped onion
2 tablespoons milk-free margarine
1 pound ground beef
1 tablespoon A-1 steak sauce
1 teaspoon salt
2 cups cooked green beans
1 can condensed tomato soup
1 can milk-free, egg-free prepared biscuits

Sauté onion in milk-free margarine. Add ground beef, A-1 sauce and salt; brown lightly. Stir in beans and soup. Pour into a 1½-quart casserole. Roll biscuits together to ¾-inch thickness. Cut with a sharp knife into small squares. Arrange the biscuit squares in two rows around the edge of the casserole with one corner of each square inserted into the meat mixture. Bake uncovered at 425 degrees for 20 minutes.
Makes 6 servings.

ONE-DISH MEAL ⊖⏚✦

2 cups sliced raw potatoes
1 cup chopped onion
1 pound ground beef
1 No. 2 can tomatoes, undrained
1 cup chopped green pepper
Salt to taste

In a greased casserole place layers of potatoes, onion, beef, tomatoes and green pepper. Season each layer to taste. Cover; bake at 250 degrees for 2 hours and 30 minutes.

Makes 6 servings.

FRANKFURTER-TOMATO SHORTCAKE ⊖⏚

½ cup chopped celery
1 cup chopped onions
½ cup chopped green pepper
¼ cup milk-free margarine
2½ cups tomatoes
8 frankfurters, sliced
Salt to taste
¾ cup flour
3 teaspoons baking powder (egg-free)
¾ cup cornmeal
2 tablespoons lard or solid vegetable shortening
1½ tablespoons water, 1½ tablespoons oil and 1 teaspoon baking powder (egg-free), beaten together
⅔ cup water

Brown celery, onions and green pepper in milk-free margarine; remove from heat. Add tomatoes, frankfurters and salt; pour into greased 2½-quart casserole. Sift flour, baking powder and 1 teaspoon salt; stir in cornmeal. Cut shortening into flour mixture; blend in the 1½ tablespoons water, oil and baking powder mixture and then blend in ⅔ cup water. Pour batter over tomato mixture in casserole. Bake uncovered at 375 degrees for 35 minutes.

BEEF AND BEAN BARBECUE

¼ cup diced green pepper
½ cup minced onion
2 tablespoons vegetable oil
1 pound ground round steak
½ cup chopped celery
1 8-ounce can tomato sauce
½ cup water
1 clove garlic, minced
2 tablespoons vinegar
1 tablespoon dry mustard
½ teaspoon thyme
1 tablespoon brown sugar
Salt and pepper to taste
1 No. 2 can (2½ cups) pork and beans

Sauté green pepper, onion and celery in oil until wilted. Add ground beef and cook, stirring, until the meat loses its color. Add tomato sauce, water, garlic, vinegar, mustard, thyme, brown sugar, and seasonings; blend well and simmer 5 minutes. Pour beans into casserole. Pour meat mixture over beans. Bake uncovered at 375 degrees for 45 minutes.

HAMBURGER STEW

2 pounds ground chuck
½ cup chopped onion
2 stalks celery, diced
Salt and pepper to taste
1 large can stewed tomatoes, undrained
1 16-ounce can mushrooms, drained
1 potato, diced
2 to 3 carrots, diced
2 cups water
2 to 3 teaspoons instant bouillon, chicken or beef flavored

Brown the meat, onion and celery and drain the fat. Season to taste. Add the remaining ingredients and bring to a boil. Cover and simmer for about 30 minutes or until the vegetables are tender.

RICE BEEF STEW

2½ pounds beef
½ cup flour
1 teaspoon salt
½ teaspoon pepper
6 tablespoons oil
½ medium onion, chopped
2 cloves garlic, minced
4 cups boiling water
3 cups canned tomatoes with their liquid
2 teaspoons salt
1 teaspoon Worcestershire sauce
18 small white onions, peeled
7 carrots, peeled and cut into 2-inch chunks
2 cups frozen peas
1 cup uncooked rice

Cut meat into 1½-inch cubes. Combine flour, salt and pepper; coat meat with flour mixture. Put oil in Dutch oven; add meat and brown in two or three batches. Add onion, garlic, boiling water, tomatoes, salt and Worcestershire sauce. Cover and simmer about 2 hours or until meat is tender. Add onions and carrots and cook 20 minutes or until vegetables are done. Add peas and rice; cook 15 minutes longer, or until rice is tender.

BEEF STEW θ ⊕ ✦

> 1 pound beef, cut in 1-inch cubes
> 2 tablespoons oil
> ¼ cup chopped onion
> 3 cups boiling water
> 1 teaspoon salt
> ⅛ teaspoon pepper
> 1 small bay leaf
> Dash of thyme
> ¾ cup diced carrots
> ¾ cup diced potatoes
> 8 to 10 small white onions
> 5 tablespoons potato starch
> 1 cup boiling water

Brown beef in oil in a large saucepan. Add onion and sauté until golden brown. Add 3 cups boiling water and seasonings; cover, and simmer 1½ to 2 hours, or until meat is tender. Add vegetables and continue cooking for 30 minutes longer, or until vegetables are done. Add a few tablespoons cold water to potato starch and mix to paste. Add to stew along with up to 1 cup boiling water, depending on amount of liquid in saucepan. Cook and stir until slightly thickened.

SPECIAL GOULASH θ ⊕ ✦

> Layer 1—1 pound ground beef, browned in skillet
> Layer 2—sliced raw potatoes
> Layer 3—sliced onions
> Layer 4—1 can kidney beans, drained
> Layer 5—1 can tomatoes with their liquid

Layer the above ingredients in a baking dish, in the order given. Season with salt and pepper to taste and a dash of garlic. Sprinkle 1 teaspoon of sugar over tomatoes. Bake at 350 degrees for about an hour, or until potatoes are done.

TAMALE PIE ⌑⌑⌑

FILLING:
- ½ cup chopped onion
- 1 pound ground beef
- 2 tablespoons oil
- 2 tablespoons chili powder
- 1½ teaspoons salt
- 1 6-ounce can tomato paste
- 1 6-ounce can water
- ½ cup sliced pitted olives
- 1 12-ounce can whole-kernel corn with sweet pepper, drained

BASE AND TOPPING:
- 3 cups water
- 1 cup cornmeal
- 1 teaspoon salt
- 1 cup cold water

Lightly brown onion and ground beef in oil in a large skillet. Stir in remaining ingredients. Simmer 10 minutes, stirring occasionally.

For base and topping: Heat the 3 cups water to boiling in a saucepan. Mix cornmeal and salt with cold water. Pour into the boiling water, stirring constantly. Bring to a boil; cook until thickened, stirring frequently. Cover; continue cooking over low heat for 5 minutes longer.

Spread half of mush into ungreased 2½-quart casserole. Spread filling over mush layer. Top with remaining mush. Bake uncovered at 400 degrees for 25 to 30 minutes.

CHILI CON CARNE

2 tablespoons salad oil
1 clove garlic, finely sliced
2 cups sliced celery
1 cup chopped onion
½ cup chopped green pepper
1 pound ground beef
1 1-pound can kidney beans, thoroughly drained
2 1-pound cans tomatoes with their liquid
½ teaspoon salt
1½ teaspoons chili powder

Heat 2 tablespoons salad oil in a 4-quart kettle and sauté garlic, celery, onion and green pepper until onion is golden brown. Add beef; stirring regularly, brown it well. Stir in kidney beans, tomatoes, salt and chili powder. Boil gently, uncovered, at least 45 minutes to blend flavors. Just before serving, taste for seasoning and add additional chili powder, salt and pepper if needed.

Makes 4 servings.

POULTRY

CHICKEN LIVER AND RICE SKILLET DINNER

¼ pound bacon
1 pound chicken livers
1 cup uncooked rice
3 tablespoons chopped parsley
2 to 3 carrots, thinly sliced
1 medium onion, thinly sliced
¼ teaspoon salt
⅛ teaspoon pepper
2½ cups water

In a medium skillet (with a tight-fitting lid), fry bacon until crispy; remove; drain; crumble. In bacon fat, in same skillet, sauté chicken livers until brown but still slightly pink in center; remove from pan. Add rice, parsley, carrots, onion, salt, pepper and water to skillet; bring to boil. Add livers; cook 25 minutes, or until rice is tender and most of water is absorbed. Sprinkle with crumbled bacon and serve.

Makes 4 servings.

ROAST TURKEY WITH FRUIT DRESSING ⊖🕀

TURKEY

    8- to 10-pound turkey
1 or 2 cloves garlic
Salt (to rub the turkey)
Melted milk-free margarine or salad oil (for greasing the turkey)
    1 medium grapefruit

FRUIT STUFFING

    4 cups toasted bread crumbs
    2 cups diced celery
    3 tablespoons grated grapefruit peel
    ½ cup crushed pineapple
    ½ cup seedless raisins
    ¼ cup chopped nuts
    ⅓ cup melted milk-free margarine
Hot water or broth to moisten
    1 teaspoon salt

Toss ingredients for stuffing together lightly and set aside.

Have turkey thoroughly clean and dry. Rub entire bird inside and out with garlic and then salt. Loosely fill bird with the stuffing, shaking to fill but do not pack. Tie and fold neck opening, tuck wings, close cavity and tie legs. Grease bird thoroughly and place breast down on V-rack. Cover with foil. Roast slowly at 325 degrees for about 3½ hours.

Turn bird breast side up and squeeze ½ of fresh grapefruit over entire bird. Leave uncovered and continue roasting 15 to 20 minutes longer. Squeeze other half of grapefruit over bird and turn up heat to 375 degrees to finish roasting and browning. After squeezing last half of grapefruit over bird, cut the tie that holds the legs together to allow this portion of the bird to brown. Finished bird should have a golden-brown skin that is crisp and faintly glazed as a result of the grapefruit and margarine. Use pan drippings and any remaining grapefruit juice to make gravy.

ROAST CHICKEN WITH SAVORY RICE DRESSING

¾ cup minute rice
2 tablespoons oil
½ cup diced celery
2 tablespoons celery leaves
2 tablespoons chopped onion
1 tablespoon chopped parsley
½ teaspoon salt
¼ teaspoon sage (optional)
Dash of pepper
1 cup chicken broth or 1 chicken bouillon cube dissolved in 1
    cup boiling water
1 small roasting chicken (3½ to 4 pounds)

Sauté rice in oil in saucepan until lightly browned, stirring constantly. Add celery, celery leaves, onion, parsley and seasonings. Sauté 2 to 3 minutes longer, then add chicken broth. Mix just to moisten all rice. Bring quickly to a boil over high heat. Cover, remove from heat, and let stand 5 minutes. Spoon into poultry cavity. Do not pack tightly. Truss as for roast turkey (page 84) and place in oven at once; roast at 350 degrees for 25 minutes a pound, or until brown and tender.

CHICKEN AND DRESSING CASSEROLE

4 cups coarsely cubed roasted or stewed chicken
4 cups chicken broth
4 tablespoons flour
4 tablespoons chicken fat

Cut up chicken and set aside. Make a gravy with the broth, flour and fat (see Meat Gravy I, page 63).

DRESSING

6 cups dried bread crumbs
½ cup melted milk-free margarine
1¼ teaspoons powdered sage
1 cup diced celery
1¼ cups broth
¾ teaspoon salt
2 tablespoons chopped onion

Mix dressing ingredients lightly with a fork.

Place dressing, chicken and gravy in layers in a casserole. Bake at 350 degrees for 35 minutes, until it is lightly browned.

BARBECUED CHICKEN

3½- to 4-pound fryer
1 cup flour
2 teaspoons salt
1 teaspoon paprika
¼ teaspoon pepper
½ teaspoon celery salt

Cut the chicken in halves, quarters or pieces. Wash, dry well and flour by shaking several pieces at a time in a bag containing the remaining ingredients. Brown on all sides in hot fat, then pour off fat, top chicken pieces with Barbecue Sauce (see below), and cook over low heat on top of stove, or bake at 325 degrees until tender, about 45 to 60 minutes.

BARBECUE SAUCE

½ cup finely chopped onion (1 medium onion)
2 tablespoons brown sugar
1 tablespoon paprika
1 teaspoon salt
1 teaspoon dry mustard
¼ teaspoon chili powder (or more as desired)
⅛ teaspoon cayenne pepper
2 tablespoons Worcestershire sauce
¼ cup vinegar
1 cup tomato juice
¼ cup ketchup
½ cup water

Mix all of the ingredients together and simmer for 15 minutes.

BAKED CHICKEN

Two 2- to 2½-pound chickens, cut up
1 cup flour
1⅓ tablespoons salt
2 tablespoons paprika
½ teaspoon pepper
¾ cup milk-free margarine
1 7-ounce jar pitted ripe olives, drained
1 cup orange juice
1 tablespoon brown sugar
½ teaspoon thyme
1 medium onion, sliced in rings

Wash chicken pieces and dry well. Combine flour, 1 tablespoon salt, 1 teaspoon paprika and the pepper in a paper bag. Put chicken in bag and shake enough to coat each piece with mixture. Brown in ½ cup milk-free margarine. Place browned chicken in a large, flat casserole. Combine ¼ cup milk-free margarine, olives, orange juice, brown sugar, 1 teaspoon salt, thyme and onion rings; simmer 4 minutes. Pour sauce over chicken. Sprinkle top of chicken with paprika. Bake uncovered 1 hour and 30 minutes to 1 hour and 45 minutes at 375 degrees or until tender. Baste 4 to 5 times during baking. Serve with hot rice if desired.

Makes 4 to 6 servings.

OVEN-FRIED CHICKEN

3 pounds chicken, cut up
1 cup crushed cornflakes
1 teaspoon salt
⅛ teaspoon pepper
⅓ cup melted milk-free margarine

Mix cornflakes, salt and pepper. Dip each piece of chicken into the melted margarine and then roll in the cornflake mixture. Place in a greased baking dish. Bake uncovered at 350 degrees for 1 hour, or until tender.

LEMON CHICKEN

1 chicken, cut up for frying
Lemon juice
Salt and pepper to taste

Clean the chicken pieces and place in a baking dish that has been slightly greased. Sprinkle the lemon juice over the chicken and season to taste. Cover and cook at 325 degrees for 1 hour. Remove the cover for the last 10 minutes of cooking.

CHICKEN AND DUMPLINGS [𝑒 ♫]

    1 stewing chicken, 5 to 6 pounds
    3 cups water
    1 sliced carrot
    1 small onion, sliced
    2 stalks celery, cut up
    1 can milk-free, egg-free prepared biscuits

Wash and clean chicken; cut into desired serving pieces. Place water in a large saucepan or a Dutch oven, add carrot, onion and celery and bring to boil. Add chicken; bring to boil. Cover; reduce heat to low, and simmer 2 to 2½ hours or until tender.

Remove chicken; strain liquid, and add water to make 2 cups. Return chicken to pot. Cut biscuits into desired bite sizes and drop one at a time on top of stew. Cover and cook for 15 minutes—don't lift cover. Serve at once.

Makes 6 servings.

CHICKEN AND RICE [𝑒 ♫ ♯]

    1 chicken, cut up for frying
Salt and pepper
    ½ cup milk-free margarine
    1 medium onion, chopped
    1 medium bell pepper, chopped
    4 chicken bouillon cubes
    1 cup raw long-grain rice
1½ cups water
    ½ teaspoon salt

Salt and pepper chicken. Brown in margarine. Sauté onion and pepper in margarine after removing chicken. Crush bouillon cubes with fork. Add to onion and pepper. Stir in rice. Add water and ½ teaspoon salt. Place in baking pan. Lay browned chicken on top of rice. Cover and bake at 250 degrees for 1½ hours.

JAMBALAYA ⟨☖☗⟩

  1½ cups cooked chicken, diced
    1 cup cooked rice
    2 cups canned tomatoes
    1 large onion, chopped
  ½ green pepper, chopped
    2 stalks celery, chopped
    4 tablespoons milk-free margarine
Salt and pepper to taste
  ½ cup bread crumbs (milk-free)

Combine chicken, rice and tomatoes in a saucepan; cook for 10 minutes. Sauté onion, green pepper and celery in milk-free margarine; add to chicken mixture. Season to taste. Pour into a greased 1½-quart casserole; cover with bread crumbs. Bake, uncovered, at 350 degrees for 1 hour.

Note: Ham or veal may be substituted for chicken.
  Makes 6 to 8 servings.

ALMOND CHICKEN AND RICE ⟨☖☗⟩

      3 cups cooked rice
      1 4-ounce can pimentoes, drained and chopped
  1½ cups cooked chicken, diced
  ¼ to ½ cup canned mushrooms
      ½ cup blanched almonds
    1¾ cups chicken broth
Salt and pepper
    1½ tablespoons instantized flour

Combine rice and pimento. Place ⅓ of rice mixture in greased casserole. Alternate layers of chicken, mushrooms and remaining rice. Top with almonds. Combine chicken broth, salt, pepper and flour. Pour over casserole. Bake at 350 degrees for 1 hour.

MAIN-DISH CHICKEN CASSEROLE ⌑

    1 4-pound stewing hen
Salt and pepper
3 to 4 celery stalks, cubed
    1 small onion
    2 cups crushed potato chips or corn chips
    ½ 8-ounce package noodles, cooked (milk- and egg-free)
    1 teaspoon minced parsley
    1 cup cooked or frozen peas
2 to 3 tablespoons chicken fat, melted
    3 tablespoons flour
Dash of paprika
    1 cup chicken broth
    8 uncooked milk- and egg-free biscuits

Stew chicken in water to cover for 3½ to 4 hours with salt, pepper, celery and onion. Chill; remove bones and cube meat. Line a greased casserole with crushed chips. Add a layer of noodles; sprinkle with 1 teaspoon salt, ⅛ teaspoon pepper and parsley. Add a layer of chicken and a layer of peas. Sprinkle with crushed chips. Repeat layers. Blend fat, flour, ¼ teaspoon salt, ⅛ teaspoon pepper and a dash of paprika in a double boiler. Stir until smooth and bubbly. Remove from heat. Stir in the liquid. Cook until thickened, stirring constantly. Pour over layers in casserole. Sprinkle with crushed chips. Bake uncovered at 350 degrees until sauce is thick and the chips are browned. Top with biscuits and bake 12 minutes longer.

Makes 6 to 8 servings.

CHICKEN AND SPAGHETTI ⊘🗲

    1 large fryer, cut up
    ¾ cup flour
    2 tablespoons oil

MARINARA SAUCE
    4 tablespoons oil
    ½ cup minced onion
    ½ cup minced green pepper
    ½ cup minced parsley
    2 6-ounce cans tomato paste
    2 teaspoons salt
    4 teaspoons vinegar
    ½ teaspoon Worcestershire sauce
    ¼ teaspoon oregano

    5 ounces spaghetti

Dip pieces of chicken in flour. Brown quickly in small amount of oil. Finish cooking chicken. Make sauce by frying the onion, pepper and parsley in the 4 tablespoons oil for about 5 minutes. Stir in the tomato paste, salt, vinegar, Worcestershire sauce and oregano. Simmer 10 minutes. Boil the spaghetti and drain. Serve chicken pieces over the spaghetti with the sauce on top.

CREAMED CHICKEN CASSEROLE ⊘🗲

    3 cups boiled noodles (egg-free) or cooked rice
    2 cups chopped boiled chicken
    ¼ cup finely chopped celery
    1 small can mushroom pieces
    1 cup thick white sauce (page 000)
    ½ cup rich chicken broth
Salt and pepper to taste
    ¾ cup bread crumbs or crackers
    4 tablespoons milk-free margarine

Combine noodles or rice, chicken, celery and mushrooms. Mix white sauce and chicken broth until smooth. Add white sauce mixture to rice mixture; blend thoroughly. Season to taste. Put in casserole. Sauté crumbs or crackers in milk-free margarine; spread over top. Bake uncovered at 350 degrees for 35 minutes.

Makes 8 servings.

CURRIED CHICKEN

½ cup slivered or chopped almonds
½ cup milk-free margarine
1⅓ cups chopped onions
1 cup diced green pepper
1 cup flour
2 tablespoons curry powder
6 cups chicken broth
1 teaspoon salt, or to taste
4 cups diced cooked chicken

Sauté almonds in margarine, remove from skillet and set aside (will be used later in rice). Add onions and green pepper to remaining margarine in skillet; sauté. Stir in flour. Gradually blend in curry powder, broth and salt. Cook until thickened, stirring occasionally. Add chicken and continue cooking until thoroughly heated. Serve over Almond-Currant Rice.

ALMOND-CURRANT RICE
2⅔ cups precooked rice
1 teaspoon salt
6 tablespoons currants
2 tablespoons milk-free margarine

Add all of the above to 2⅔ cups boiling water. Cover, remove from heat and let stand for 5 minutes. Stir in almonds reserved from Curried Chicken recipe, above. Serve.

ORIENTAL CHICKEN CASSEROLE

3 cups toasted bread crumbs (crumbs from milk-free bread)
2 cups bean sprouts
⅔ cup sliced water chestnuts
½ cup chopped or sliced mushrooms
1 teaspoon salt
2 cups diced cooked chicken
¼ cup sugar
2 tablespoons cornstarch
¾ cup pineapple juice
¼ cup soy sauce
2 tablespoons vinegar
¼ cup toasted almonds

Combine bread crumbs, bean sprouts, water chestnuts, mushrooms, salt and chicken in a mixing bowl.

In a small saucepan combine sugar and cornstarch. Add pineapple juice and soy sauce to sugar and cornstarch. Bring to a boil over medium heat, stirring constantly. Cook 5 minutes or until thick. Remove from heat and add vinegar.

Place chicken mixture in a greased 1½-quart casserole. Pour sauce mixture over chicken and top with toasted almonds. Bake in a 350-degree oven for 30 minutes.

Makes 6 servings.

CHICKEN CACCIATORE

1 clove garlic, mashed
1 large onion, sliced
2 tablespoons oil
4 to 5 pounds chicken, cut into pieces
1 6-ounce can tomato paste
1 cup hot water
Salt and pepper
½ cup sliced mushrooms (fresh or canned)
½ cup dry red wine (optional)

Cook garlic and onion in oil. Add chicken and brown on all sides. Combine tomato paste, water, salt, pepper; pour over chicken. Cover and cook over low heat until tender, about 45 minutes. Add mushrooms and wine (optional). Cook 5 minutes more.
Makes 6 servings.

BISCUIT-TOPPED CHICKEN PIE

3 tablespoons milk-free margarine
3 tablespoons flour
1 teaspoon salt
3 cups chicken broth
2 cups diced cooked chicken
1 cup mixed vegetables (drained)
2 tablespoons diced onion
½ teaspoon pepper
1 can milk-free and egg-free prepared biscuits

In a saucepan, melt margarine. Add flour and salt. Add chicken broth slowly and bring to a boil. Place chicken, vegetables, onion, and pepper in a 2-quart casserole dish. Pour hot broth mixture over chicken and vegetables. Top with biscuits. Bake uncovered at 425 degrees for 30 minutes. Serve hot.

PORK

PORK CHOP–MUSHROOM CASSEROLE ⊖🎜

    6 pork chops
    1 2½-ounce can sliced mushrooms
2½ cups cooked peas
    2 tablespoons flour
Salt to taste

Brown chops in skillet, place in casserole. Drain mushrooms, reserving liquid. Cover chops with peas and mushrooms. Remove all but 2 tablespoons fat from skillet. Blend in flour. Combine reserved liquid with enough water to make 1½ cups. Gradually stir liquid into flour mixture. Add salt to taste. Cook until thickened, stirring constantly. Pour sauce over casserole ingredients, cover, and bake at 350 degrees for 1 hour.
    Makes 4 to 6 servings.

BROWN RICE–PORK CHOP CASSEROLE ⊖🎜♯

    1 cup brown rice
    2 tablespoons milk-free margarine
    2 beef bouillon cubes
    2 cups boiling water
    4 pork chops
Salt and pepper to taste

Sauté rice in margarine for 2 or 3 minutes, stirring constantly. Add bouillon cubes to boiling water; stir until dissolved. Pour over rice. Pour rice mixture into casserole. Bake covered at 300 degrees for

30 minutes. Season pork chops and brown in frying pan used for rice. Place browned pork chops on top of rice; cover closely and continue baking until chops are tender, about 1 hour.

Makes 4 servings.

BAKED PORK CHOPS

6 pork chops, cut ¾ inch thick
1 teaspoon salt
2 cups boiling water
2 tablespoons A-1 Sauce
2 tablespoons flour
¼ cup cold water
½ cup rolled bread crumbs or cracker crumbs

Brown chops on both sides in hot frying pan. Remove to greased baking dish. Add salt, water and A-1 Sauce to pan and heat. Thicken with flour mixed with ¼ cup cold water. Stir until smooth. Pour over chops, top with bread crumbs and bake 45 minutes at 350 degrees.

BAKED PORK CHOPS NORMANDE

4 to 6 loin pork chops
Salt and pepper to taste
3 large apples, thinly sliced
2 teaspoons sugar
2 teaspoons cinnamon
1 tablespoon milk-free margarine
1 large bay leaf
2 tablespoons grated onion
3 whole cloves
½ cup bouillon

Trim fat from chops; season with salt and pepper. Place in greased baking dish; cover with thin slices of cored, pared apples.

(continued)

Sprinkle mixture with sugar, cinnamon and milk-free margarine. Add remaining ingredients. Cover and bake at 400 degrees for 1 hour and 30 minutes. Remove cover and cook 10 to 15 minutes longer, or until brown.

Makes 4 to 6 servings.

PORK CHOP CASSEROLE

5 pork chops
1 teaspoon salt
1/8 teaspoon pepper
1 No. 2 can baked beans
1 cup chili sauce
1 tablespoon brown sugar
1 teaspoon Worcestershire sauce
1 medium green pepper

Brown pork chops on both sides; season with salt and pepper. Place chops in a 3-quart greased casserole. Combine baked beans, chili sauce, brown sugar and Worcestershire sauce. Pour over pork chops. Garnish with green pepper rings. Bake at 375 degrees for 1 hour.

Makes 5 to 6 servings.

PORK CHOPS WITH TOMATO SAUCE

6 pork chops
Salt and pepper to taste
1 small onion, sliced
2 8-ounce cans tomato sauce (with mushrooms or plain)

Brown pork chops in pan, using a small amount of oil to keep them from sticking, if necessary. Season to taste. Place browned pork chops into casserole dish. Put slices of onion over tops. Pour tomato sauce over all. Cover and bake in 350-degree oven for 1 hour.

Makes 3 to 6 servings.

GLAZED PORK CHOPS ⊖⊞✦

4 pork chops
1 orange, peeled and cut into 4 horizontal slices
1 apple, peeled and cut into 4 horizontal slices
Cinnamon
Ground cloves
1 can beef broth
1 tablespoon brown sugar
1 tablespoon cornstarch
2 tablespoons orange juice

In skillet, brown chops on both sides; pour off drippings. Top each with slice of orange and apple, sprinkle with cinnamon and cloves. Add the beef broth and brown sugar. Cover and cook over low heat for 35 minutes or until tender. Stir cornstarch into orange juice till smooth; gradually blend into the braising liquid. Cook, stirring constantly, until slightly thickened; simmer a few minutes longer and serve.

PORK CHOPS AND PINEAPPLE ⊖⊞✦

6 pork chops
¾ cup canned sliced mushrooms
6 slices of pineapple
½ cup mushroom liquid
1 cup pineapple juice
Salt and pepper to taste

Brown pork chops in skillet. Remove from pan. Drain mushrooms and reserve liquid. Brown pineapple quickly and remove from pan. Brown mushrooms and remove from pan. Place pork chops in pan, and put a slice of pineapple on each chop. Cover with mushrooms and juices; season to taste. Cover pan and cook on low heat 1 hour. Serve hot.

STUFFED PORK CHOPS [⌀ ⏢]

6 pork chops, cut 1 inch thick
1 cup bread crumbs (egg-free and milk-free)
½ cup chopped apple
½ teaspoon sage
¼ teaspoon thyme
Salt and pepper to taste
2 tablespoons melted milk-free margarine
3 tablespoons water or stock

Make a horizontal slit in each chop to form a pocket for the stuffing. Combine bread crumbs, chopped apple and seasonings; stuff the chops loosely and secure with toothpicks. Sprinkle chops with salt and pepper and brown in margarine on both sides in hot skillet. Add water or stock to cover bottom of pan. Cover and simmer over very low heat or bake at 350 degrees for 45 minutes, or until tender. Turn chops occasionally, adding a little water if needed.

OLD SOUTH CASSEROLE [⌀ ⏢ ⚹]

6 medium sweet potatoes
½ cup chopped pecans
1 cup cubed cooked ham
1½ cups pineapple juice
¼ cup sugar
¼ cup brown sugar
1 tablespoon cornstarch
2 tablespoons milk-free margarine

Wash potatoes and boil until tender. Peel and cut in half lengthwise. Place in greased (using milk-free margarine) baking dish with pecans and ham. Mix pineapple juice, sugars, cornstarch and milk-free margarine; pour over potatoes. Bake uncovered at 300 degrees for 1 hour. Baste several times during baking with syrup in dish.
Makes 6 servings.

JELLY-GLAZED HAM ⊖⊕✦

1½-inch slice ready-to-eat ham (approximately 2 pounds)
Whole cloves
½ cup currant or apple jelly
1 tablespoon vinegar
½ teaspoon dry mustard
¼ teaspoon cinnamon
⅛ teaspoon ground cloves

Insert whole cloves in the fat around the edges of the ham at 2-inch intervals. Place slice in shallow baking dish and bake at 325 degrees for 30 minutes. Meanwhile, make jelly glaze: Heat jelly over low heat, stirring until smooth; add remaining ingredients. Remove ham from oven. Spoon half the glaze over ham and return to oven; bake 10 minutes. Spoon on remaining glaze; bake 10 minutes longer or until well glazed.

Makes 4 servings.

HAM AND BARBECUE SAUCE ⊖⊕

1 2-pound slice of smoked ham
¼ cup chopped onions
½ clove garlic, minced
¼ cup ketchup
2 tablespoons Worcestershire sauce
¼ cup cider vinegar
1 10½-ounce can tomato soup
2 teaspoons milk-free margarine
1 teaspoon brown sugar
⅛ teaspoon pepper

Combine onions and garlic with remaining ingredients and pour over ham. Cover and bake at 350 degrees for 1 hour or until tender.

HAWAIIAN HAM θ♁♀

Ready-to-eat ham
1 tablespoon prepared mustard
1 can pineapple rings; drain and reserve syrup
Whole cloves

Spread mustard over the ham and place in a baking dish. Pour pineapple syrup (¾ to 1 cup) over ham and stick with the cloves. Bake in a 350-degree oven until heated through (about 1 hour). Arrange pineapple rings on ham. Continue baking until pineapple is brown, basting frequently with juices around ham.

PINEAPPLE, MARSHMALLOW HAM θ♁♀

8 average slices of baked ham
1 small can chunk pineapple
16 large marshmallows

Put ham slices in baking dish, pour chunks of pineapple and juice over ham. Bake at 350 degrees for 10 minutes, then put marshmallows over top and put back into oven until marshmallows melt and begin to brown.

AMERICAN CHOP SUEY θ♁♀

½ pound pork or chicken, diced
2 medium onions, finely chopped
2 tablespoons oil
1 medium green pepper, finely chopped
3 medium mushrooms, finely chopped (optional)
1 cup diced celery
1½ teaspoons salt
1 cup meat stock
2 cups cooked rice

Brown meat and onion in oil. Add green pepper, mushrooms, celery, salt and meat stock. Cook uncovered over low heat until all is tender. Serve hot on rice.

Makes 6 servings

SOUTH SEA CASSEROLE

1 can pork and ham luncheon meat or leftover ham
1 tablespoon cornstarch
1 cup water
⅓ cup pineapple juice
1 tablespoon vinegar
½ teaspoon Worcestershire sauce
1 teaspoon soy sauce
¼ teaspoon mustard
1 9-ounce can pineapple tidbits, drained
1 tomato, cut in sixths
½ green pepper, seeded and sliced
½ cup chopped celery
3 cups cooked rice

Cut meat into ¾-inch cubes; brown lightly in skillet. Combine cornstarch, liquids and seasonings. Add to meat; cook until mixture thickens, stirring constantly. Add remaining ingredients except rice; simmer 5 minutes. Serve over rice.

Makes 4 servings.

SEAFOOD

OVEN-FRIED FISH FILLETS I

Melt ½ cup milk-free margarine. Dip fish serving pieces in this, then in cornflake crumbs. Place on foil and bake at 400 degrees for 20 minutes.

OVEN-FRIED FISH FILLETS II

1½ pounds cod or haddock fillets, fresh or frozen
2 tablespoons lemon juice
¼ cup flour
½ teaspoon salt
½ cup melted milk-free margarine
1 cup cornflake crumbs

Thaw fillets if frozen. Rinse, pat dry, and cut into serving portions. Combine lemon juice, flour, salt, and milk-free margarine, stirring into a smooth paste. Dip fish in paste; coat well with cornflake crumbs. Arrange in single layer on foil-lined baking pan. Bake 20 minutes in a 400-degree oven or until fish flakes easily with a fork.

Makes 6 servings.

HALIBUT BAKED IN FOIL ⊖⊕❋

2 fresh halibut steaks, cut ¾ inch thick (about 1 pound)
2 tablespoons salad oil
4 medium potatoes, thinly sliced
4 medium onions, thinly sliced
2 carrots, thinly sliced
Salt and pepper to taste
Parsley

Preheat oven to 450 degrees. With a sharp knife, remove skin from the halibut steaks. Cut meat away from bone and halve, lengthwise, into 4 servings. For each serving: Pour ½ tablespoon salad oil in center of an 18-inch square of heavy-duty foil. Top with 1 piece of fish, then 1 thinly sliced potato, 1 thinly sliced onion and ½ thinly sliced carrot, sprinkling between each layer salt and pepper to taste. Wrap and place on cookie sheet. Bake 25 minutes, or until fish flakes easily with a fork and vegetables are tender. Sprinkle with snipped parsley.

Makes 4 servings.

TUNA PIE ⊖⊕

1¼ cups diced potatoes
¼ cup diced celery
1 tablespoon chopped onion
¾ cup frozen or canned peas
1 7-ounce can flaked tuna (1 cup)
¾ teaspoon salt
⅛ teaspoon pepper
1 tablespoon flour
Baking Powder Biscuits (page 147)

Cook potatoes, celery, and onion in small amount of salt water until tender. Drain. Reserve ½ cup liquid. Combine vegetables and tuna. Pour into greased 1-quart casserole. Add seasonings. Gradually add vegetable liquid to flour; blend until smooth. Pour over tuna and vegetables. Arrange biscuits on top and bake at 400 degrees for 20 minutes.

INDIVIDUAL TUNA CASSEROLES ⌀⌗

　　3 cups water
　　3 chicken-flavored bouillon cubes
　　¼ cup flour
　　1 teaspoon salt
　　¼ cup cold water
　　1 cup cooked peas
　　1 4-ounce can sliced mushrooms
　　2 7-ounce cans tuna packed in water
　　6 small cooked onions
　Unbaked Pie Crust (page 223) or Baking Powder Biscuits (page
　　147)

Bring 3 cups water to a boil in a 2-quart saucepan. Remove from heat. Stir in chicken bouillon cubes. Make smooth paste of flour, salt and ¼ cup cold water. Add to chicken stock and cook over low heat until thick, stirring constantly, about 5 minutes. Drain peas, mushrooms and tuna. Flake tuna. Add to the thickened stock and continue cooking for about 2 minutes or until tuna mixture is heated thoroughly. Place an onion in each of 6 well-greased 10-ounce casseroles. Portion tuna filling into casseroles and top with pie crust or biscuits. Bake at 425 degrees for 30 minutes or until crust is golden brown.

SWEET-AND-SOUR SHRIMP ⌀⌗✦

　　1 pound cooked, peeled, deveined shrimp
　　1 medium onion, thinly sliced
　　1 small green pepper, cut into 1-inch squares
　　¼ cup melted milk-free margarine or cooking oil
　　2 8¼-ounce cans pineapple chunks in heavy syrup

½ cup white vinegar
¼ cup sugar
2 tablespoons cornstarch
1 tablespoon soy sauce
½ teaspoon dry mustard
¼ teaspoon salt
⅔ cup cherry tomato halves or thin tomato wedges
3 cups hot, cooked rice
½ cup toasted, slivered almonds

Cut large shrimp in half; if small leave whole. Cook onion and green pepper in milk-free margarine until tender, but not brown. Drain pineapple and reserve syrup. Combine pineapple syrup, vinegar, sugar, cornstarch, soy sauce, dry mustard and salt; shake together until well blended; add to cooked vegetables. Cook, stirring constantly, until thick and clear. Gently stir in pineapple chunks, tomatoes and shrimp, and heat thoroughly. Combine cooked rice and almonds. Serve sweet-and-sour mixture over rice.
Makes 6 servings.

SHRIMP AND CRAB CASSEROLE

1 pound shrimp (2 cups)
1 pint crab meat (2 cups)
½ cup ketchup
2 tablespoons Worcestershire sauce
1 teaspoon Tabasco
¾ cup cracker crumbs
½ green pepper, finely chopped
½ onion, finely chopped

Boil shrimp 3 to 5 minutes; peel. Combine crab meat, ketchup, Worcestershire sauce, Tabasco and cracker crumbs in medium-sized bowl. Add the green pepper and onion. Place shrimp in casserole dish. Cover with crab mixture and bake at 350 degrees for 30 minutes.

SEAFOOD NEWBURG ⎡ ⊝🕀 ⎤

1 small can shrimp
1 can crab meat
2 cans tuna
1 tablespoon minced onion
1 tablespoon lemon juice
1 tablespoon Worcestershire sauce
Dash of Tabasco
½ teaspoon dry mustard
2 cups medium white sauce (page 64)
¾ cup crushed cornflakes
¼ cup melted milk-free margarine

Drain and flake all seafood and place in a greased casserole. Add onion, lemon juice, Worcestershire, Tabasco and dry mustard to white sauce; pour over fish. Combine cornflakes and milk-free margarine. Cover fish with mixture. Bake uncovered for 20 minutes at 425 degrees.

Makes 4 servings.

SEVEN SEAS CASSEROLE ⎡ ⊝🕀 ⎤

1¼ cups cream-of-mushroom soup substitute (page 31)
1¼ cups water (part nondairy creamer, if desired)
¼ cup chopped onion (optional)
¼ teaspoon salt
1⅓ cups instant rice
1 6½-ounce can tuna, salmon or lobster
1 box *thawed* frozen peas
Paprika (optional)

Combine soup, water, onion, and salt; bring to boil. Pour half into greased 1½-quart casserole. In layers, add rice, seafood, peas. Pour remaining soup over; sprinkle with paprika, if desired. Cover. Bake at 375 degrees for 20 minutes.

FISH LOAF OR CAKE ⟨🖊🕮⟩

1¼ cups riced potato
¾ cup cooked flaked fish
¼ teaspoon pepper
1½ teaspoons salt
1 tablespoon grated onion
2 tablespoons chopped pickle (optional)

Mix together the above ingredients. Shape into loaf to bake or into cakes to fry. The cakes may be rolled into potato meal. Bake the loaf at 350 degrees for 30 minutes. Pan-fry the cakes in melted fat until brown on both sides and thoroughly heated through, about 5 minutes on each side.

SHRIMP CREOLE ⟨🖊🕮⟩

½ cup chopped onion
⅔ cup chopped celery
⅔ cup chopped green pepper
2 tablespoons melted milk-free margarine
1 tablespoon flour
¾ teaspoon salt
⅛ teaspoon cinnamon
⅛ teaspoon nutmeg
Dash of pepper
1 1-pint 2-ounce can tomato juice
1 8-ounce can tomato sauce
½ teaspoon Worcestershire sauce
1½ tablespoons vinegar
1½ teaspoons brown sugar
2 pounds shrimp, cooked and shelled
Hot cooked rice

Sauté onion, celery and green pepper in milk-free margarine until tender. Combine flour, salt, cinnamon, nutmeg and pepper; stir into onion mixture. Gradually add tomato juice and tomato sauce. Add Worcestershire sauce, vinegar and brown sugar. Simmer for 15 to 20 minutes. Add shrimp and heat. Serve over rice.

Makes 8 servings.

VEGETARIAN

STUFFED PEPPERS

1¼ cups whole kernel corn, fresh, frozen or canned
1¼ cups diced tomatoes, fresh or canned
¼ cup chopped celery
2 tablespoons chopped onion
⅔ cup soft bread crumbs
1 teaspoon salt
⅛ teaspoon pepper
3 large green peppers
2 tablespoons milk-free margarine

Mix together the corn, tomatoes, celery, onion, bread crumbs, salt and pepper. Cut the green peppers in half lengthwise; clean out seeds and wash. Parboil in salted water for 5 minutes. Pile corn mixture in pepper halves. Dot with milk-free margarine. Place in a shallow pan. Bake uncovered at 375 degrees for 40 to 45 minutes.

Vegetables

K. Callahan

BASIC VEGETABLE COOKING

BROILED

Arrange vegetables such as halved tomatoes, marinated eggplant slices or mushroom caps on a shallow baking dish and place under preheated broiler. Baste with milk-free margarine, flavored sauce or sugar glaze. Broil until lightly browned.

BOILED

Cook, covered, in a small amount of water until tender.

BAKED

Place whole vegetable in heated oven and cook until tender; or grate or cut vegetable into small pieces and bake covered.

FRIED

Brown vegetable in oil. Certain vegetables, such as onion rings and eggplant, are good when dipped into a batter and then deep-fried. Use water or a nondairy liquid creamer with a little oil to dip the vegetable in and then roll it in cornmeal that has been seasoned or flour that has been seasoned or a mixture of both.

STEAMED

Place vegetables on a rack over vigorously boiling water with the vegetable surrounded with steam. Cover tightly.

PRESSURE-COOKED

Cook vegetables by following the instructions that came with your pressure cooker.

ASPARAGUS

ASPARAGUS ALMANDINE

¼ cup slivered blanched almonds
¼ cup milk-free margarine
¼ teaspoon salt
2 teaspoons lemon juice
2 cups cooked asparagus, drained

Sauté almonds in margarine until golden, stirring occasionally; remove from heat. Add salt and lemon juice; pour over hot asparagus. Let stand for a few minutes before serving.

BEANS

BEST BAKED BEANS

5 slices bacon, crisply fried and crumbled
2 16-ounce cans baked beans, drained
½ green pepper, seeded and chopped
½ medium onion, chopped
1½ teaspoons prepared mustard
½ cup ketchup
½ cup hickory-smoke barbecue sauce
½ cup brown sugar, firmly packed

Mix all ingredients in a saucepan. Cover and simmer over very low heat for 45 minutes.

EASY BAKED BEANS

2 16-ounce to 18-ounce cans pork and beans
¾ cup brown sugar, firmly packed
1 teaspoon dry mustard
6 slices bacon, cut in pieces
½ cup ketchup

Empty 1 can pork and beans into bottom of greased casserole. Combine sugar and mustard; sprinkle half of mixture over beans. Top with remaining beans. Sprinkle rest of sugar-mustard mixture, chopped bacon and ketchup over beans. Bake, uncovered, at 325 degrees for 30 minutes.

Makes 8 servings.

ZESTY BUTTER BEANS

2 tablespoons chopped onion
2 tablespoons chopped green pepper
1 tablespoon milk-free margarine
1 10½-ounce can tomato soup
¼ cup water
1 tablespoon brown sugar
1 tablespoon vinegar
1 tablespoon mustard
2 1-pound cans butter beans, drained

Sauté onion and green pepper in margarine; add remaining ingredients except beans and bring to a simmer. Place the beans in an oiled 1-quart casserole. Cover with sauce. Bake at 375 degrees for 45 minutes.

GREEN BEANS AND POTATOES

½ to 1 pound fresh green beans
2 to 3 small potatoes
Salt and pepper to taste
½ teaspoon sugar
Pinch of thyme
3 pieces bacon
1 medium onion, sliced

Clean and snap beans. Wash potatoes and cut up. Place about 2 cups of water in a large saucepan; add the seasonings, bacon and onion and then the beans and potatoes. Bring to a boil and cover. Simmer for about 20 to 30 minutes or until vegetables are tender.

BEETS

BEETS WITH ORANGE SAUCE

½ cup sugar
2 tablespoons cornstarch
⅛ teaspoon salt
1 cup orange juice
1 tablespoon milk-free margarine
3 cups cooked diced beets

Combine dry ingredients; add orange juice and margarine. Cook for 5 minutes in top of double boiler or over very low heat in saucepan. Add beets and let stand for several hours. Reheat just before serving.

BAKED BEETS 〔θ ⊕ ✿〕

16 medium-sized fresh beets
¼ cup sugar
¾ teaspoon salt
¼ teaspoon paprika
1 tablespoon lemon juice
3 tablespoons milk-free margarine
1 medium-sized onion, grated
⅓ cup water

Peel and slice or finely chop beets; place in greased 7-inch baking dish. Add sugar, salt, paprika and lemon juice. Dot with margarine and onion; add water. Cover and bake at 400 degrees for 30 minutes or until tender, stirring twice.

PANNED BEETS 〔θ ⊕ ✿〕

6 medium-sized beets, peeled
1 teaspoon salt
2 tablespoons milk-free margarine
3 tablespoons vinegar
3 tablespoons water

Shred beets. Simmer, covered, with salt, margarine, vinegar and water until tender.

BROCCOLI

BROCCOLI WITH ALMOND-LEMON SAUCE

1 bunch or 1 package chopped broccoli, cooked
¼ cup milk-free margarine
2 tablespoons lemon juice
1 tablespoon grated lemon rind
¼ cup slivered almonds

Drain broccoli. Blend margarine, lemon juice and rind and almonds. Pour over hot broccoli; serve.

ALMONDS AND BROCCOLI

1 clove garlic, crushed
⅓ cup milk-free margarine
¼ cup chopped almonds
⅔ cup sliced and pitted olives
2 teaspoons lemon juice
2 packages frozen broccoli, cooked

Cook garlic in margarine over medium heat for 2 minutes, stirring occasionally; add nuts, olives and lemon juice. Heat thoroughly; sprinkle over hot broccoli.

CABBAGE

CRUNCHY CABBAGE

1 medium-sized fresh cabbage
2 tablespoons salt
8 cups boiling water
4 tablespoons melted milk-free margarine
½ teaspoon pepper

Remove outside leaves of cabbage; cut into quarters. Remove core; cut into ¼-inch shreds. Place in a large pot of rapidly boiling salted water; cover. Allow to boil rapidly for 3 minutes; turn off heat. Let stand for 3 minutes on burner. Cabbage should be crisp and crunchy. Uncover; drain. Add margarine and pepper; serve immediately.

GERMAN BAKED CABBAGE

1 small onion, chopped
¾ cup cracker crumbs
½ cup milk-free margarine
1 small cabbage, chopped and cooked

Sauté onion and cracker crumbs in margarine. Alternate layers of cabbage and crumbs in casserole. Sprinkle water over this, if needed. Bake at 350 degrees for 20 minutes or until heated through.

CONFETTI CABBAGE

1 cup chopped celery
1 green pepper, chopped
1 medium onion, chopped
2 tablespoons milk-free margarine
2 cups shredded cabbage
Salt and pepper to taste

Sauté celery, green pepper and onion in margarine; add cabbage. Cover and simmer for 10 to 15 minutes, stirring occasionally. Salt and pepper to taste.

RED CABBAGE

6 strips bacon, diced
1 2-pound head red cabbage, shredded
1 apple, diced
4 tablespoons water
4 tablespoons sugar
2 teaspoons salt
Pepper to taste
6 to 8 tablespoons vinegar or red wine

Brown bacon in a saucepan. Add cabbage, apple and water, Cover tightly; simmer slowly about 1 hour. Stir often to prevent burning. Add sugar, salt, pepper and vinegar; stir. Serve warm. Will keep in refrigerator for several days

CARROTS

TOASTED CARROTS

6 medium carrots, scraped
1 teaspoon sugar
¼ cup melted milk-free margarine
1 cup cracker crumbs

Place carrots in saucepan with sugar and enough water to prevent scorching. Cook, covered, for 15 to 20 minutes or until carrots are just tender. Roll each carrot in melted margarine and cracker crumbs. Toast under broiler for 3 to 5 minutes, turning so all sides are lightly browned.

LEMON-GLAZED CARROTS

1½ pounds medium-sized carrots
¼ teaspoon salt
¼ cup milk-free margarine
2 tablespoons sugar
4 thin slices lemon

Wash carrots and pare. Place in a large saucepan with salt and enough boiling water to cover; simmer, covered, 15 minutes, or until tender. Drain. Melt milk-free margarine in a large skillet. Stir in sugar, lemon slices and carrots; cook over medium heat, stirring occasionally, until carrots are glazed.
Makes 6 servings.

HONEYED CARROTS

> 4 to 5 carrots, peeled
> 1 tablespoon honey
> 3 whole cloves
> 2 tablespoons milk-free margarine
> Dash of salt

Slice carrots about ⅛ inch thick. Put honey, cloves, margarine, salt and small amount of water in saucepan. Add carrots; cook until tender.

BAKED SHREDDED CARROTS

> 4 medium carrots, peeled
> Salt and pepper to taste
> 2 tablespoons milk-free margarine

Grate carrots with medium grater. Place carrots in well-greased (using milk-free margarine) casserole. Season and dot with milk-free margarine. Cover and bake at 325 degrees for about 25 minutes.

CARROT AMBROSIA

> 12 small carrots, cooked
> ¼ cup milk-free margarine
> ¼ cup sugar
> 2 oranges, sliced

Glaze carrots in mixture of margarine and sugar. Add oranges and heat. This is best prepared in advance so that the orange flavor penetrates the carrots. Reheat before serving.

CAULIFLOWER

CAULIFLOWER AND BROCCOLI POLONAISE

1 large cauliflower (about 2 pounds)
Boiling water
Salt
3 lemon slices
1 bunch fresh broccoli (about 1½ pounds)
¾ cup milk-free margarine
⅔ cup bread crumbs
3 tablespoons lemon juice

Trim leaves and stem from cauliflower. Place, stem side down, in large kettle. Cover with boiling water. Add 1½ teaspoons salt and lemon slices. Bring to a boil; reduce heat; simmer, covered for 20 to 25 minutes, or until tender. Drain. Wash and trim leaves from broccoli. Using a vegetable peeler, remove tough outer skin from stalks. If stalks are very large, split lengthwise, through flowers and all. Arrange in single layer in bottom of large skillet. Pour ½ cup boiling water over broccoli; sprinkle with ½ teaspoon salt. Cook, covered, over medium heat 8 to 10 minutes, or until stalks are just tender and water is evaporated. Meanwhile, slowly heat ¼ cup milk-free margarine in a large skillet. Add bread crumbs and sauté, stirring, until golden brown. Remove crumbs, and set aside. In same skillet, melt remaining milk-free margarine with lemon juice. Drain broccoli and cauliflower. Pour lemon butter over vegetables. Sprinkle with browned bread crumbs.
Makes 6 servings.

CORN

FRIED CORN

¼ cup milk-free margarine
3 medium onions, sliced
1 12-ounce can whole-kernel corn, drained
¼ cup chopped green pepper
½ teaspoon salt
1 tablespoon chopped pimento

Melt margarine in saucepan; add onions. Cover and simmer for 3 to 4 minutes or until half done. Add corn, green pepper and salt. Cook until heated through. Toss with pimento just before serving.

CORN AND BROCCOLI DISH

½ cup milk-free margarine
1 12-ounce can whole-kernel corn with red and green sweet peppers, drained
1 10-ounce package frozen chopped broccoli, thawed and drained
1 teaspoon basil leaves
½ teaspoon salt
⅛ teaspoon garlic powder
⅛ teaspoon pepper

In a heavy 2-quart saucepan melt the margarine. Add remaining ingredients; stir to blend. Cover; cook over medium heat, stirring occasionally, until crisply tender, about 8 to 10 minutes.

EGGPLANT

EGGPLANT WITH TOMATO

$1\frac{1}{2}$ cups cubed eggplant
2 tablespoons chopped green pepper
2 tablespoons chopped onion
Bacon fat
1 cup canned tomatoes
Salt and pepper
2 slices bacon, chopped
Cracker crumbs, browned in milk-free margarine

Soak eggplant in salt water for about 30 minutes; cook in boiling water until tender. Brown green pepper and onion in bacon fat; add tomatoes and eggplant. Place in casserole; add salt, pepper and bacon. Sprinkle cracker crumbs over all. Bake at 400 degrees for about 15 minutes.

STUFFED EGGPLANT

1 eggplant
Salt and pepper
2 tablespoons milk-free margarine
$\frac{1}{2}$ cup water
2 cups cracker crumbs

Halve eggplant lengthwise; scoop out center pulp, leaving $\frac{1}{2}$-inch rind. Cover shells with cold water. Finely chop pulp; season with salt and pepper. Sauté in margarine for 10 minutes, stirring constantly; add water and 1 cup crumbs. Drain shells; sprinkle inside with salt and pepper. Fill with eggplant mixture; top with remaining crumbs. Place halves in baking dish one-third full of hot water. Bake at 350 degrees for 30 minutes.

MUSHROOMS

MUSHROOMS AND WILD RICE

2 10½-ounce cans condensed beef broth
1 cup finely sliced onions
½ cup wild rice
1 cup uncooked white rice
2 cups sliced fresh mushrooms
⅓ cup milk-free margarine
Chopped parsley

Cook together for 20 minutes the beef broth, sliced onions and wild rice in a covered 1¾-quart casserole over medium heat. Remove from heat, add white rice, and bake, covered, at 400 degrees for 20 minutes. Remove casserole from oven. Allow to stand for 20 minutes before removing cover.

Meanwhile, sauté mushrooms in margarine for 5 minutes, stirring often. Combine mushrooms and pan juices with cooked rice and toss with a fork. Place in serving dish and sprinkle with chopped fresh parsley.

ONIONS

APPLES AND ONIONS 🖉🗄

    9 medium onions
    6 medium apples
  16 slices bacon, cooked and crumbled
  ¾ teaspoon salt
    1 cup water
  ½ cup cracker crumbs
    2 tablespoons bacon fat

Peel and thinly slice onions and apples; layer with bacon in greased casserole. Sprinkle each layer with salt; add water. Sauté crumbs in bacon fat; sprinkle over casserole. Bake, covered, at 375 degrees for 30 minutes. Uncover, bake for 15 minutes longer.

ONION WRAPPED IN BACON 🖉🗄🗄

  6 medium onions
  6 teaspoons milk-free margarine
  6 slices bacon
  1 cup brown sugar

Skin onions and score tops; place 1 teaspoon of milk-free margarine on top of each. Wrap each onion in a slice of bacon; fasten with toothpicks. Arrange onions in center of double 14-inch square of foil. Top with brown sugar; close foil. Cook on grill on low heat for 30 minutes or until onions are tender.

PEAS

BLACK-EYED PEAS

1 package fresh black-eyed peas
3 slices bacon
½ onion, diced
Seasonings to taste
Pinch of sugar

Place all of the above ingredients in a saucepan. Cover with water and bring to a boil. Cover and simmer for about 1 hour or until tender.

STEAM-FRIED PEAS

2 slices bacon, diced
1 small onion, chopped
2 tablespoons milk-free margarine
2 cups shelled fresh peas
2 tablespoons water

Sauté bacon and onion in margarine; add remaining ingredients. Simmer, covered, for about 20 minutes or until tender

FRENCH PEAS 🌀🏵🌿

> 1½ tablespoons milk-free margarine
> 2 tablespoons water
> ½ cup thinly sliced mushrooms
> 1½ cups fresh peas
> 1 small onion, thinly sliced
> ½ teaspoon salt

Combine all ingredients in pan; cook over medium heat for 12 to 16 minutes or until peas are tender, shaking pan occasionally.

Note: One 10-ounce package frozen peas may be used. Cook for 5 to 15 minutes.

CHRISTMAS PEAS 🌀🏵🌿

> ¾ cup finely chopped onion
> ¼ cup finely chopped green pepper
> 2 tablespoons minced pimento
> 1 tablespoon minced parsley
> ½ bay leaf
> 3 tablespoons milk-free margarine
> ⅛ teaspoon nutmeg
> ½ teaspoon salt
> ½ teaspoon vinegar
> Pinch of sugar
> 2 10-ounce packages frozen peas, cooked

Sauté onions, green pepper, pimento, parsley and bay leaf in margarine for 10 minutes or until tender; remove bay leaf. Add nutmeg, salt, vinegar and sugar; stir into hot drained peas. Serve.

PEAS AND POTATOES

1 10-ounce package frozen peas
1 potato, diced
½ onion, diced
Seasonings to taste
Pinch of sugar

Place peas and potato and onion in saucepan and add enough water to cover. Season to taste and add the pinch of sugar. Bring to boil and simmer, covered, for about 20 minutes, or until vegetables are tender.

RICE AND PEA RING

1 tablespoon salt
4 teaspoons milk-free margarine
2 cups instant rice
1 package frozen peas
2 tablespoons chopped pimento

Bring 2 cups water, salt and margarine to a boil; stir in rice. Cover; remove from heat. Let stand for 5 minutes; fluff with fork. Cook peas according to package directions; drain. Combine peas and pimento with rice; press into 5½-cup ring mold. Cover with foil; set in pan of hot water. Bake at 250 degrees until thoroughly heated. Unmold; fill center with creamed meat.

PEAS AND WATER CHESTNUTS

½ cup chicken broth
1 package frozen peas
8 water chestnuts, sliced
1 tablespoon milk-free margarine
½ teaspoon salt

Bring broth to a boil; add peas and water chestnuts. Simmer for 3 minutes; add margarine and salt.

POTATOES

QUICK-BAKE POTATOES

6 medium potatoes, cut into ¼-inch slices
1 teaspoon salt
½ teaspoon garlic powder
4 tablespoons milk-free margarine

Place potatoes in a 2-quart casserole or baking pan; sprinkle with salt and garlic powder and dot with margarine. Cover with foil and seal. Bake at 350 degrees for 30 minutes.

Note: Potatoes can be crisped by placing under the broiler for 5 to 10 minutes, stirring once or twice to crisp more evenly.

PANNED POTATOES

4 thick slices onion
2 tablespoons oil
4 potatoes, thinly sliced
Seasonings to taste

Sauté onion in oil until transparent; remove from pan. Sauté potatoes in oil until partially done, stirring occasionally. Return onions to pan. Cook, covered, until potatoes are tender. Add small amount of water as needed; season to taste.

POTATOES AND MUSHROOMS

½ pound mushrooms, sliced
½ cup chopped onion
3 tablespoons milk-free margarine
1 teaspoon salt
Dash of pepper
4 cups cooked mashed potatoes (using water and more milk-free margarine instead of milk or cream)
1 tablespoon chopped parsley

Sauté mushrooms and onion in margarine for 8 minutes or until tender; season with salt and pepper. Fold in seasoned mashed potatoes. Sprinkle with parsley.

SPANISH POTATOES ⟨symbols⟩

4½ to 5 cups potatoes, cut into ½-inch cubes
1 cup potato stock
1 slice ham, ½ inch thick
¼ cup minced onion
¼ cup minced green pepper
¼ cup chopped pimento
Salt to taste
1 teaspoon paprika

Simmer potatoes in salted water until barely tender; drain and reserve water. Measure liquid; add water to make 1 cup. Sauté ham; cube. Sauté onion, pepper and pimento in ham drippings; add extra fat if needed. Stir in potatoes, ham, salt, paprika and potato stock; simmer for 30 minutes.

PIQUANT POTATOES ⟨symbols⟩

2 tablespoons chopped onion
2 tablespoons diced green pepper
3 tablespoons milk-free margarine
½ cup chopped cooked ham or bacon
2 cups cooked cubed potatoes
2 tablespoons chopped pimento
Salt and pepper

Sauté onion and green pepper in margarine until tender. Add remaining ingredients; heat.

CALICO POTATOES

4 cups thinly sliced potatoes
1 cup thinly sliced carrots
½ to 1 onion, sliced (optional)
1 cup cubed or sliced celery
Bacon drippings
2 cups cooked or canned tomatoes
½ teaspoon savory salt
2 teaspoons salt
½ teaspoon prepared mustard
½ teaspoon celery salt
4 slices bacon, cooked and crumbled

Cook potatoes, carrots, onion and celery in bacon drippings for 10 to 12 minutes; turn carefully to distribute fat. Add tomatoes and seasonings. Cook until potatoes are tender. Sprinkle bacon over top.

SOUPY POTATOES

Milk-free margarine
Thinly sliced potatoes
1 can beef-vegetable soup
Seasonings to taste

Grease the bottom of a casserole with the milk-free margarine. Place the potatoes in a thick layer on the bottom. Pour one-third of the can of soup over the potatoes. Add more potatoes and soup until the casserole is full. Sprinkle with seasonings. If more liquid is needed, add water. Dot generously with milk-free margarine. Cover and bake at 350 degrees until potatoes are done.

SPINACH

FRESH SPINACH 〔𝛳𝛽✳〕

1 package fresh spinach
Salt and pepper
¼ cup milk-free margarine

Rinse and pick over the spinach leaves, discarding large stems. Bring a large pot of water to a boil; add spinach and cook for 3 to 6 minutes. Drain at once; place in a heated serving dish and add margarine and seasonings.

SAVORY CREAMED SPINACH 〔𝛳𝛽〕

1 package fresh spinach
3 strips bacon
1 small onion, finely chopped
1½ tablespoons flour
Salt and pepper to taste

Cook spinach by placing it in a saucepan and bringing it to a boil and then simmer until done. Lift out with a fork; chop fine with two knives. Sauté bacon; remove from pan. Sauté onion in fat. Brown flour; add spinach and ½ cup water. Stir constantly until thickened. Add water until desired consistency. Reduce heat; cook for 15 minutes. Return crumbled bacon to pan; season to taste.

SPINACH AND BACON [θ ₿]

> 2 10-ounce packages frozen spinach
> 8 strips bacon
> 2 tablespoons minced onion
> 1½ cups coarse bread crumbs
> ⅓ cup vinegar
> 2 tablespoons water
> 2 tablespoons sugar

Cook spinach in boiling salt water as directed on package; drain and chop into bite-sized pieces. Dice bacon into skillet; fry until crisp. Remove from pan; add to spinach. Pour off all but 3 tablespoons bacon fat. Sauté onion in fat until clear; add bread crumbs. Toast, stirring constantly, until golden brown. Add spinach, bacon, vinegar, water and sugar. Stir until well blended.

SQUASH

CORN CHIP SQUASH [θ ₿ ✦]

> 4 or 5 medium squash, diced
> ¼ cup minced onion
> 1 tablespoon minced pimento
> Salt and pepper to taste
> 1 tablespoon milk-free margarine
> 1 ¾-ounce package corn chips, crushed

Cook squash in small amount of water until tender; add onion and pimento. Season with salt, pepper and margarine. Place in margarine-greased dish; sprinkle corn chips over top. Bake at 350 degrees for 25 to 30 minutes.

BAKED ACORN SQUASH ⌷θ☗✿⌷

    2 medium acorn squash
    2 to 4 tablespoons milk-free margarine
    Salt
    Pepper (optional)
    2 to 4 tablespoons brown sugar

Wash squash. Cut in halves lengthwise; remove seeds and stringy parts. Place halves, cut side down, in shallow pan. Bake at 400 degrees for 30 minutes. Turn cut side up; sprinkle with margarine, salt, pepper if desired, and brown sugar. Bake at 400 degrees for 30 minutes or until tender.

GOLDEN SQUASH ⌷θ☗✿⌷

    3 acorn squash, halved
    6 teaspoons melted milk-free margarine
    6 teaspoons honey, maple syrup or brown sugar
    Chopped dates and pecans (optional)
    Pineapple and honey (optional)
    Raisins and finely chopped apple (optional)
    Salt to taste

Remove seeds and stringy portion from squash; place, cut side down, in shallow pan with water ¼ inch deep. Place in preheated oven at 350 degrees. When water has evaporated, turn squash cut side up. Brush cavity generously with margarine; add 1 teaspoon honey in each. Stuff with date, pineapple or apple mixture. Sprinkle with salt. Continue baking until tender.

SPICED SQUASH ⟨☺♙♣⟩

    2 acorn or butternut squash, cooked
    ¼ cup milk-free margarine
    1 teaspoon salt
    ½ teaspoon cinnamon (optional)
    ¼ cup brown sugar

Mash hot squash with margarine, seasonings and brown sugar. Place in a 2-quart casserole. Bake at 350 degrees for 50 minutes.

SQUASH CASSEROLE ⟨☺♙♣⟩

    6 cups cubed yellow squash
    2 teaspoons salt
    1 teaspoon pepper
    1 tablespoon sugar
    ½ cup milk-free margarine, softened
    ½ cup sliced green onions or scallions
    1 pound link or bulk sausage
    3 baking apples, sliced 1 inch thick
    6 teaspoons brown sugar
 3 to 4 tablespoons water (optional)

Preheat oven to 400 degrees. Spread squash evenly in a greased 9 × 13-inch baking dish. Combine salt, pepper and sugar; sprinkle over squash. Dot with margarine; add onion slices. Cut sausage into 1-inch lengths or shape into 1-inch balls. Partially cook sausage; drain fat. Place sausage in casserole. Add apples; sprinkle with brown sugar. Add water if squash is dry; cover tightly with foil. Bake in 400-degree oven for 30 minutes. Remove foil; reduce heat to 350 degrees. Continue baking for 20 minutes or until brown and squash is tender.

Note: If precooked squash is used, omit steaming process and bake for 35 to 40 minutes.

STUFFED ZUCCHINI ⊘⊞

4 zucchini, trimmed
2 tablespoons minced onion
2 tablespoons milk-free margarine
1 slice bread, finely shredded
½ cup cooked tomatoes
Salt and pepper

Cook zucchini in boiling salted water for 10 to 12 minutes. Cut in half lengthwise; scoop out soft center and place in bowl. Add all remaining ingredients to squash pulp; mix well. Fill zucchini shells with mixture. Place in small, shallow pan. Bake at 350 degrees for 15 minutes.

ITALIAN ZUCCHINI ⊘⊞❋

2 tablespoons olive oil
6 to 8 medium zucchini squash, cut into ¼-inch slices
1 clove of garlic, minced
1 medium onion, sliced
4 or 5 peeled tomatoes
1 teaspoon salt
Italian seasoning (optional)
Dash of pepper

Heat oil in skillet; add zucchini, garlic and onion. Cook until almost tender. Add tomatoes and seasonings. Cook on medium heat for 10 minutes.

FRIED SQUASH $\theta\oplus\ast$

1 firm long yellow or green squash, thinly sliced
¼ cup cornmeal
½ teaspoon salt
Few dashes of pepper
2 tablespoons cooking oil

Dip squash into mixture of cornmeal, salt and pepper. Sauté squash in hot oil until a delicate brown, turning once. Add more oil if necessary.

TOMATOES

FRIED GREEN TOMATOES $\theta\oplus$

4 or 5 medium green tomatoes
⅓ cup flour
¾ teaspoon salt
Dash of pepper (optional)
¼ cup shortening

Wash tomatoes; remove stem end. Cut crosswise into ½-inch slices. Blend flour, salt and pepper; dip tomato slices into mixture. Brown quickly in fat on one side; turn. Reduce heat; cook until soft in center.

STEWED OKRA AND TOMATOES

5 slices of bacon
1 large onion, chopped
1 medium green pepper, chopped
1 to 2 pounds okra, cut up
1 to 2 pounds tomatoes, peeled and chopped
1 teaspoon salt
½ teaspoon pepper
1 teaspoon sugar

Fry bacon in skillet until brown; remove from skillet. Sauté onion and pepper in bacon fat for 5 minutes; add okra and cook 2 minutes longer, stirring constantly. Add tomatoes and seasonings, cover and simmer for 10 to 15 minutes. Place in serving dish and garnish with bacon slices.

RICE AND TOMATOES

1 small onion, chopped
2 tablespoons cooking oil
1 cup uncooked rice
2 cans clear chicken broth
1½ teaspoons salt
¼ teaspoon pepper
3 medium tomatoes or 1 large can of tomatoes, drained
¼ cup milk-free margarine
1 teaspoon garlic salt
½ teaspoon oregano
1 teaspoon sugar

Sauté onion in oil until tender; add rice, chicken broth, 1 teaspoon salt and pepper. Bring to boil. Reduce heat; simmer, covered, for 25 minutes. Peel and slice tomatoes ½ inch thick; sauté in margarine with garlic salt for 4 minutes. Sprinkle with remaining salt, oregano and sugar; add to rice.

BACON-STUFFED TOMATOES 🖊️

4 tomatoes
3 slices bacon
1 tablespoon minced onion
¾ cup plus 2 tablespoons soft bread crumbs
1 tablespoon melted milk-free margarine
Salt and pepper to taste

Wash tomatoes, slice off stem end. Scoop out pulp. Fry bacon crisp; remove from pan. Sauté onion in bacon fat for 3 minutes; add ¾ cup crumbs, crumbled bacon and tomato pulp. Season. Fill tomatoes with mixture; top with margarine and 2 tablespoons crumbs. Bake at 375 degrees for 20 minutes or until tender and crumbs are brown.

ORIENTAL TOMATO SKILLET 🖊️

2 tablespoons vegetable oil
½ cup chopped onion
2 medium unpared zucchini squash, quartered
3 medium tomatoes, cut into wedges
1 3-ounce can sliced mushrooms, drained
¼ teaspoon salt
¼ teaspoon curry powder
¼ teaspoon ginger
Dash of pepper

Heat oil in a wok or skillet; add onion and zucchini. Stir-fry over medium heat for 5 minutes; stir in remaining ingredients. Cook, covered, for 5 minutes longer or until vegetables are tender but slightly crisp.

YAMS AND SWEET POTATOES

QUICK CANDIED YAMS

3 to 4 medium yams, peeled and halved
⅓ cup melted milk-free margarine
1 cup brown sugar
½ cup water
6 to 8 large marshmallows, halved (optional)

Place yams in margarine in large skillet; sprinkle with sugar. Add water. Cover and cook over medium heat for 20 minutes or until yams are tender, basting occasionally. Add marshmallows the last 5 minutes.

YAMS AND ORANGE

5 large yams, cooked and sliced
½ cup plus 2 tablespoons brown sugar
1 tablespoon melted milk-free margarine
2 unpeeled oranges, sliced thin
½ cup orange juice
¼ cup honey
¼ cup bread crumbs

Place layer of yams in a casserole that has been greased with milk-free margarine; sprinkle with brown sugar and dot with margarine. Cover with oranges. Repeat layers until all is used, using ½ cup brown sugar. Pour orange juice and honey over layers. Combine bread crumbs with remaining brown sugar; sprinkle over layers. Dot with additional margarine. Bake, covered, at 350 degrees for 45 minutes. Uncover and bake 15 minutes longer.

SWEET POTATO–PINEAPPLE SURPRISE ⬚

3 cups cooked mashed sweet potatoes
2 tablespoons milk-free margarine
½ teaspoon salt
¾ cup crushed pineapple, well drained
6 large marshmallows
Crushed cornflakes

Combine sweet potatoes, margarine and salt; fold in pineapple. Mold mixture around each marshmallow to form a ball; roll in cornflakes. Place in greased baking dish. Bake at 350 degrees for 30 to 40 minutes.

Makes 6 servings.

SWEET POTATO–HONEY BALLS ⬚

2½ cups mashed cooked or canned sweet potatoes
¾ teaspoon salt
Dash of pepper
4 tablespoons melted milk-free margarine
½ cup miniature marshmallows
⅓ cup honey
1 cup chopped pecans

Combine potatoes, salt, pepper and 2 tablespoons margarine; stir in marshmallows. Chill; shape into balls, using ¼ cup potato mixture for each. Heat 1 tablespoon margarine with honey in small, heavy skillet; add potato balls, one at a time. Carefully but quickly coat each with glaze, using two forks. Roll in nuts; place separately in greased shallow casserole. Drizzle with remaining margarine. Bake at 350 degrees for 15 to 20 minutes.

Makes 10 servings.

SWEET POTATO–CEREAL PUFFS

8 sweet potatoes, cooked and mashed
1 teaspoon salt
2 tablespoons milk-free margarine
½ cup brown sugar
Crushed cornflakes or crisp rice cereal
12 marshmallows

Combine sweet potatoes with salt, margarine and sugar; form into balls. Roll in crushed cereal; place in baking pan. Top with marshmallows. Bake at 350 degrees for 15 minutes or until done. *Makes 12.*

Breads

QUICK BREADS

TOMATO-FLAVORED HUSH PUPPIES

1 cup cornmeal
½ cup flour
½ teaspoon salt
½ teaspoon garlic salt
1 medium onion, finely chopped
½ No. 2 can tomatoes, chopped
Oil for deep frying

Stir cornmeal, flour, salt and garlic salt together thoroughly. Add chopped onion. Add enough chopped tomatoes to make semi-thin mixture. Drop by spoonfuls into hot shortening, about 375 degrees, and cook till brown, turning once. If fat is too hot, hush puppies will brown on outside before getting done in the middle.

Makes 4 to 6 servings.

SOUTHERN CORN PONE

⅓ teaspoon salt
¼ cup cornmeal
½ cup boiling water

Preheat oven to 400 degrees. Mix dry ingredients and stir in boiling water. Drop in a generously oiled baking pan. Bake until brown, about 8 minutes.

Makes 4 small cakes.

BAKING POWDER BISCUITS

> 1 cup all-purpose flour
> ¼ teaspoon salt
> 2 teaspoons baking powder (egg-free)
> 1½ to 2 tablespoons lard or solid vegetable shortening
> ⅓ cup water

Preheat oven to 400 degrees. Sift flour with salt and baking powder. Cut in the shortening with a pastry blender or two knives. Add the water and mix just until flour is moistened. Turn onto lightly floured surface; knead for 30 seconds. Roll ¼ inch thick. Cut into rounds with a 2-inch cookie cutter and place 1 inch apart on a greased baking sheet. Bake for 12 to 15 minutes.
Makes 12 to 14 biscuits

7-UP BISCUITS

> 2 cups flour, sifted
> 1 teaspoon salt
> 4 teaspoons baking powder (egg-free)
> ½ cup solid shortening
> ¾ cup 7-Up
> Melted milk-free margarine

Preheat oven to 450 degrees. Sift dry ingredients into bowl; cut in shortening until mixture resembles coarse cornmeal. Add 7-Up all at once; stir briskly with fork until dry ingredients are evenly moistened. Turn onto lightly floured surface; knead quickly 10 times. Roll to ¾-inch thickness. Allow to rest for 5 minutes. Cut with lightly floured 2-inch cutter. Arrange on baking sheet. Brush lightly with melted milk-free margarine. Bake for 10 to 12 minutes or until golden brown.
Makes 12.

RYE BAKING-POWDER BISCUITS ☐

1 cup unsifted rye flour
1½ teaspoons baking powder (egg-free)
¼ teaspoon salt
3 tablespoons shortening
3 to 4 tablespoons water

Preheat oven to 450 degrees. Grease baking sheet. Sift together the rye flour, baking powder and salt. Cut in shortening until mixture is like coarse cornmeal. Stir in 3 to 4 tablespoons water to form thick, pliable dough. Turn onto lightly rye-floured board; roll about ½ inch thick. Cut with 2-inch cutter; place on baking sheet; bake 12 to 15 minutes.
Makes 6.

UPSIDE-DOWN ORANGE BISCUITS ☐

¼ cup milk-free margarine
½ cup orange juice
¾ cup sugar
2 teaspoons grated orange rind
2 cups flour
½ teaspoon salt
3 teaspoons baking powder (egg-free)
⅓ cup shortening
¾ cup water
½ teaspoon cinnamon

Preheat oven to 450 degrees. In a small saucepan, combine milk-free margarine, orange juice, ½ cup of sugar and orange rind. Cook 2 minutes; pour into 12 muffin tins. Combine flour, salt, and baking powder. Cut in shortening with a pastry blender or 2 knives until mixture resembles coarse cornmeal. Stir in water and mix with a fork just until moistened. Knead for 30 seconds. Roll out ¼ inch thick.

Mix cinnamon and remaining ¼ cup sugar; sprinkle over dough. Roll as for jelly roll. Slice 1 inch thick; place cut side down in muffin tins. Bake for 15 to 20 minutes.

Makes 12.

CORN BREAD

1 cup cornmeal
1 cup flour
¼ cup sugar
5 teaspoons baking powder (egg-free)
½ teaspoon salt
1 cup plus 2 tablespoons water
⅓ cup oil

Preheat oven to 425 degrees. Combine all ingredients and beat well. Bake in a greased and floured 8-inch cake pan for 20 to 25 minutes.

Makes 8 servings.

APRICOT-ALMOND BREAD

1½ cups dried apricots
3 tablespoons soft milk-free margarine
1½ cups sugar
2 cups flour, sifted
2 teaspoons baking powder (egg-free)
½ teaspoon salt
½ teaspoon baking soda
⅓ cup water
½ cup coarsely chopped almonds

Preheat oven to 350 degrees. Simmer apricots in water to cover for 5 minutes. Drain fruit, reserve juice. Chop apricots. Cream margarine with sugar; stir in ½ cup reserved apricot juice. Sift flour with baking powder, salt and baking soda. Stir dry ingredients into creamed mixture alternately with water, stirring batter only until blended. Fold in almonds. Pour batter into greased 9 × 5-inch bread pan; bake for 1 hour or until done.

Note: This bread slices more easily if allowed to stand overnight.

ORANGE NUT BREAD

2¼ cups oat flour or ground oatmeal
4 teaspoons baking powder (egg-free)
¼ teaspoon baking soda
¾ cup sugar
¾ teaspoon salt
¾ cup chopped nuts (optional)
2 tablespoons oil
¾ cup orange juice
1 tablespoon grated orange rind

Preheat oven to 350 degrees. Grease and flour (using oat flour) a 9 × 5-inch loaf pan. Sift together the dry ingredients. Add nuts, oil, orange juice and orange rind; stir until all is moistened. Pour into pan. Bake 1 hour.

BANANA NUT BREAD

½ cup oil
1 cup sugar
3 tablespoons oil, 3 tablespoons water and 2 teaspoons baking powder (egg-free), beaten together
2 bananas, mashed
2 cups flour
1 teaspoon baking soda
¼ cup nuts, chopped

Preheat oven to 350 degrees. Mix all ingredients in the order given. Pour into a greased and floured 9 × 5-inch loaf pan and bake for 40 to 50 minutes.

PUMPKIN BREAD

1⅔ cups flour
1 teaspoon baking powder (egg-free)
1 teaspoon baking soda
¾ teaspoon salt
½ teaspoon cinnamon
¼ teaspoon cloves
1⅓ cups sugar
⅓ cup oil
3 tablespoons oil, 3 tablespoons water and 2 teaspoons baking powder (egg-free), beaten together
1 cup puréed pumpkin
⅓ cup water

Preheat oven to 350 degrees. Sift together flour, baking powder, baking soda, salt and spices. Beat sugar, oil and the 3 tablespoons oil, 3 tablespoons water and 2 teaspoons baking powder mixture. Add pumpkin. Mix thoroughly. Slowly add flour mixture and water. Beat until thoroughly mixed. Pour into greased and floured 9 × 5-inch loaf pan. Bake for 1 hour.

Note: ¼ cup chopped nuts may be added if desired.

YEAST BREADS

WHITE LOAF BREAD

2 tablespoons dry yeast
2½ cups warm water
3 tablespoons oil
4 tablespoons honey or molasses
1½ teaspoons salt
5½ to 6 cups flour

Dissolve the yeast in the warm water. Add the oil, honey and salt. Beat in enough flour to form a medium-soft dough, turn out on a floured board and knead about 8 to 10 minutes, or until smooth and elastic, adding a little more flour if needed. Cover and let rise until doubled (about 1½ hours). Push down. Shape the dough into 2 loaves. Place in oiled loaf pans and allow to rise again until double in bulk.

Bake 10 minutes at 400 degrees. Reduce heat to 350 degrees and bake 30 minutes more. Cool on racks.

SOURDOUGH BREAD

STARTER
1 package yeast
2 cups warm water
2 cups flour

Dissolve yeast in water; add flour and mix well. Cover with a cloth and set in warm place for 2 or 3 days, or until until a pleasantly sour odor develops and the starter is bubbly. Put ½ cup starter in scalded pint jar; cover tightly. Store in a cool place or refrigerate for future use.

DOUGH

4 cups flour
2 tablespoons sugar
1 teaspoon salt
2 tablespoons oil

Mix dry ingredients in a bowl, making a well in the center. Combine remaining starter and oil; pour into the well in flour. Mix well, adding more flour if necessary to make a soft dough. Knead on a floured board for 10 minutes. Place in a greased bread pan; let rise in a warm place for 2 hours or until light. Bake at 275 degrees for 50 to 60 minutes.

Note: To use stored sourdough starter, combine ½ cup starter with 2 cups warm water and 2 cups flour; beat well. Set in a warm place for 6 to 8 hours or overnight. Reserve ½ cup for future starter. The bread will not be distinctly sour until the starter has been in use for a time. The recipe can be varied by substituting 1 cup whole wheat for 1 cup white flour. Honey, brown sugar or molasses may be used instead of sugar.

HOT ROLLS

1 package dry yeast
1 teaspoon salt
2 tablespoons sugar
2½ cups warm water
½ cup melted shortening
5 cups unbleached flour (approximately)

Combine yeast, salt, sugar and water. Add the shortening and beat in flour, a cup at a time, until a medium-soft dough is formed. Turn out onto a floured surface and knead until smooth and elastic, about 10 minutes. Place dough in a greased bowl, cover with a towel, and let rise in a warm place until doubled (1 hour or more). Punch the dough down, turn out on a floured work surface and let rest for 20 minutes. Shape into rolls. Place on greased baking sheet, cover with a towel and let rise again until light, 45 minutes to 1 hour. Bake in a preheated 400-degree oven for 20 to 25 minutes, or until golden brown.

OATMEAL BREAD

2 cups boiling water
1 cup oatmeal
2 tablespoons milk-free margarine
2 tablespoons wheat germ (optional)
2½ teaspoons salt
½ cup molasses
2 packages dry yeast
⅓ cup warm water
6 cups flour

In a large bowl, pour the boiling water over the oatmeal. Stir and let stand for 20 minutes. Near the end of the 20 minutes, add margarine, wheat germ, salt and molasses and in the last 5 minutes, combine the yeast and warm water in a separate bowl and let the yeast mixture sit for 5 minutes. Pour yeast into the oatmeal mixture and add 2 cups flour, stir well and add 2 more cups of flour, mix until mixture comes away from the bowl. Knead the last 2 cups of flour in on a floured board. Knead for 10 to 15 minutes.

Put the kneaded dough into a greased bowl, cover with a towel and set in a warm place until it doubles in size (about 2 hours). Punch down and shape it into 2 loaves and let rise in greased bread pans until double in size (about 2 hours).

Bake at 325 degrees for 40 to 50 minutes. When the loaves are done there will be a hollow sound when you thump them. Brush tops with margarine.

BRAN LOAF BREAD

3 tablespoons milk-free margarine
3 tablespoons dark brown sugar
2 tablespoons molasses
2 teaspoons salt
1 cup bran
1½ cups boiling water
1 package dry yeast
¼ cup warm water
5 to 5½ cups flour

Put first 5 ingredients in a large bowl, add boiling water and blend. Let cool to room temperature. Meanwhile, dissolve yeast in warm water. Beat 1 cup flour into bran mixture, add yeast and beat until smooth. Add remaining flour. Knead for 15 minutes. Let rise, covered, for 2 hours. Punch down and divide in half, shape into loaves and place in greased loaf pans. Let rise until double in bulk. Bake 50 minutes at 325 degrees. When brown, brush tops with melted milk-free margarine.

RICE- AND RYE-FLOUR BREAD

1⅓ cups rye flour
⅔ cup rice flour
½ teaspoon salt
2 tablespoons sugar
10 teaspoons baking powder (egg-free)
2 teaspoons oil
1⅓ cups water

After sifting dry ingredients together, add oil and water, mixing well. Grease bread pan with oil and bake at 350 degrees for 40 minutes. Makes 1 loaf.

BREAD STICKS

1 package yeast
⅔ cup warm water
1 teaspoon salt
1 tablespoon sugar
¼ cup soft shortening
2 cups flour, or as needed

Dissolve yeast in water. Add salt, sugar, shortening and half of flour. Beat vigorously until smooth. Mix in remaining flour. Knead on floured board until smooth. Cover; let rise 1 hour or until doubled. Divide dough in half. Cut into 24 pieces. Roll into pencil shapes of desired thickness. Place on greased baking sheet 1 inch apart. Bake at 400 degrees for 20 to 25 minutes.

LIMPA (SWEDISH RYE BREAD)

2 cups boiling potato water
5 to 6 cups rye flour
3 medium potatoes, mashed
1 cup molasses, heated
1 cake yeast
3 cups lukewarm water
2 teaspoons salt
1 cup raisins
Grated rind of 2 oranges
2 teaspoons fennel seed
3 tablespoons vegetable oil
6 to 8 cups white flour

Pour potato water over 3 cups rye flour and work with a wooden spoon until well moistened. Mix in the potatoes and molasses; cover and let cool. Meanwhile, combine yeast, water, salt and enough of the remaining rye flour to make a sponge. Let the sponge rise, covered, in a warm place for 45 minutes to 1 hour, or until light. Beat potato mixture into sponge and add the orange rind, fennel seed and

oil. Beat in white flour, a cup at a time, until dough is stiff enough to handle. Turn the dough out on a well-floured kneading surface and knead for 5 to 8 minutes, or until elastic (it will still be slightly sticky). Place in a large greased bowl, turning to grease all surfaces of the dough; cover and let rise until doubled (about 2 hours). Shape into loaves and place in greased loaf pans or on baking sheets. Cover with towels and let rise for 1 hour. Bake at 425 degrees for 15 minutes. Reduce heat to 350 degrees; continue baking for 50 minutes.
Makes 4–5 loaves.

NEVER-FAIL SWEET RYE BREAD

⅓ cup molasses
⅓ cup white corn syrup
½ cup brown sugar
2 cups apple juice (or another juice)
2 tablespoons shortening
1 tablespoon salt
2 packages yeast
½ cup warm water
2 cups rye flour
2 cups white flour

Scald and cool molasses, corn syrup, brown sugar, juice and shortening. Add salt. Dissolve yeast in warm water and add to cooled molasses mixture. Stir in flour to make a stiff dough. Let rise until doubled in bulk. Knead well, using as little additional flour as possible. Shape into two loaves and place in greased loaf pans. Cover and let rise until doubled in bulk. Bake at 425 degrees for 30 minutes; reduce heat to 325 degrees and continue baking for 35 minutes. Place on rack to cool.

CARDAMOM RAISIN BREAD

1 package yeast
½ cup plus 2 teaspoons sugar
2¼ cups lukewarm water
1 tablespoon salt
1 tablespoon (heaping) shortening
6 to 8 cups flour
2 cups raisins
1 tablespoon cardamom

Dissolve yeast with 2 teaspoons sugar in ¼ cup lukewarm water. Combine ½ cup sugar, salt, shortening and 2 cups water. Add yeast mixture; stir. Add enough flour to form stiff dough. Knead until smooth. Add raisins and cardamom; knead until blended well. Let rise until double in bulk. Work down and let rise until double again. Shape into 2 loaves. Place in greased loaf pans; let rise until double in bulk. Bake at 425 degrees for 10 minutes; reduce heat to 350 degrees and bake 50 minutes.

Cakes, Cookies, Pies and Dessert Sauces

CAKES

APPLESAUCE FRUIT CAKE

3 cups strained applesauce, sweetened or unsweetened
2 cups sugar
1 cup milk-free margarine
4½ cups flour
4 teaspoons baking soda
1 teaspoon nutmeg
2½ teaspoons cinnamon
1 teaspoon salt
½ teaspoon cloves
2 cups dates
½ cup each nuts, candied cherries and candied pineapple
2 cups raisins

Combine the applesauce, sugar and margarine in a saucepan, bring to a boil, reduce heat and simmer for 5 minutes. Let stand overnight.

Butter two 9 × 5-inch loaf pans and line with waxed paper. Sift together the flour, soda, nutmeg, cinnamon, salt and cloves. Chop the dates, nuts, cherries and pineapple and combine with raisins. Dredge the fruits with a little of the flour mixture.

Stir flour and spices into the applesauce, mixing well; fold in the fruits and nuts. Fill prepared pans two-thirds full. Bake in a slow, 250-degree oven for 2 or 3 hours, or until a toothpick inserted in the center of the cake comes out clean.

Note: You may add up to twice as much fruit if you desire a fruity cake.

CHRISTMAS FRUIT CAKE 　⊖🛢

    2 cups (½ pound) dried pears
    4 cups water
    1 cup dried apricots
    2 cups water
    3 cups flour
    ½ teaspoon salt
    ¼ cup oil
    1 cup toasted and chopped walnuts
    1 teaspoon vanilla
    Rind and juice of 1 orange

Place dried pears and 4 cups water in a saucepan. Cover and simmer for ½ hour. Purée. Place apricots and 2 cups water in a saucepan. Cover and simmer for ½ hour. Chop. Combine flour and salt.

    Preheat oven to 375 degrees. Mix the oil into the flour mixture. Add the pear purée, chopped apricots, walnuts, vanilla and orange rind. Add enough orange juice to make a moist batter. Pour into a greased and floured loaf pan. Bake for 2 to 2½ hours.

FRUITY CAKE 　⊖🛢

    ½ cup milk-free margarine
  1⅓ cups sugar
    1 teaspoon vanilla
    3 cups sifted flour
    1 teaspoon salt
    5 teaspoons baking powder (egg-free)
  1¼ cups liquid (any fruit juice, such as lemon juice and grated lemon rind, or pineapple juice and a small amount of crushed pineapple, or orange juice and some orange rind)

Preheat oven to 350 degrees. Cream margarine and sugar. Add vanilla. Sift dry ingredients together and add alternately with liquid.

Pour into two 8-inch cake pans that have been greased and then lined with waxed paper and greased again. Bake at 325 to 350 degrees for 30 minutes. Let rest for 5 minutes and then turn out. Frost with no-cook white icing that you have added the same juice to in place of water, so that the icing will have the same flavor.

APPLESAUCE SPICE CAKE

½ cup solid shortening
½ cup granulated sugar
½ cup sifted rye flour
1½ cups sifted barley flour
3 teaspoons double-acting baking powder (egg-free)
1 teaspoon baking soda
1 teaspoon salt
½ teaspoon cinnamon
¼ teaspoon nutmeg
½ cup minus 1 tablespoon canned sweetened applesauce
Sifted confectioners' sugar

Preheat oven to 350 degrees. Grease bottom of a 9-inch square cake pan; line with waxed paper; grease and flour (with barley flour) the paper. In a medium bowl, cream the shortening and sugar until light and fluffy. Sift together the flours, baking powder, baking soda, salt, cinnamon and nutmeg. Beat one-third of the flour mixture into the shortening-sugar mixture until smooth; beat in the applesauce until smooth. Beat in another third of the flour mixture. Beat until smooth. Then beat in remaining one-third of flour mixture. Beat 1 minute. Turn into cake pan; smooth surface. Bake 30 to 35 minutes, or until cake pulls away from the sides. (The center of this cake will not be as firm as a regular cake.) Let cake cool for ½ hour; turn out. Serve sprinkled with sifted confectioners' sugar.

FRUIT AND SPICE CAKE

1 cup water
2 cups raisins
1 cup brown sugar, firmly packed
½ cup solid shortening
⅛ teaspoon nutmeg
½ teaspoon cinnamon
½ teaspoon allspice
½ teaspoon salt
2 cups sifted flour
1 teaspoon baking soda
1 teaspoon double-acting baking powder (egg-free)
1 cup chopped pecans (optional)
Sifted confectioners' sugar

Combine the water, raisins, brown sugar, shortening, spices and salt in a saucepan and bring to a boil; simmer, uncovered, for 3 minutes. Grease a 9 × 9 × 2-inch square cake pan. Preheat oven to 375 degrees. Sift together the flour, baking soda and baking powder. Stir together the raisin mixture, flour mixture and the pecans. Beat until smooth, about 1 minute. Pour into pan and bake for 35 to 40 minutes or until cake comes away from the pan. Cool about 15 minutes, then turn out. Cool completely; sprinkle with sifted confectioners' sugar. Cut into 16 squares.

SPICY SUGAR CAKE

1½ cups potato flour
½ teaspoon baking soda
¾ cup potato meal
4½ teaspoons baking powder (egg-free)
½ teaspoon salt
3 teaspoons cinnamon
½ teaspoon allspice
½ cup oil
3 cups granulated sugar
¾ cup brown sugar
2¼ cups mashed potatoes, sieved and warm
1½ teaspoons vanilla
½ cup cocoa powder

Preheat oven to 350 degrees. Sift the first seven ingredients; set aside. Cream oil and sugars, add potato and vanilla. Beat well. Add dry ingredients, mixing enough to blend well, a little at a time, beating well after each addition. Line an oblong cake pan with aluminum foil and smooth the dough into this. Top with cocoa. Bake for 45 to 50 minutes.

ORANGE BLOSSOM CAKE

½ cup milk-free margarine
¾ cup sugar
2 teaspoons vanilla
1 tablespoon finely grated orange peel
3 cups sifted flour
1½ teaspoons salt
4 teaspoons double-acting baking powder (egg-free)
1¼ teaspoons baking soda
½ cup orange juice
½ cup plus 2 tablespoons water

Preheat oven to 350 degrees. Lightly grease two 8-inch layer-cake pans; line with waxed paper, then lightly grease and flour the paper. In a medium bowl, cream together the margarine and the sugar until light and fluffy. Beat in the vanilla and orange peel. Sift together the flour, salt, baking powder and baking soda. Beat one-third of the flour mixture into the sugar mixture; beat in the orange juice until smooth. Add another third of the flour mixture and the water; then beat in remaining third of the flour mixture. Beat at medium speed for 1 minute. Divide between pans; spread evenly, then push batter slightly up around edges. Bake for 30 to 35 minutes, or until cake comes away from the pan. Let cool on cake rack about 30 minutes before turning out. Remove carefully.

OLD-FASHIONED CHEWY CAKE

1 cup raisins
1 cup chopped dates
1 cup sugar
1 cup hot water
2½ tablespoons solid vegetable shortening
1½ cups flour
½ teaspoon baking soda
1 teaspoon cinnamon
½ teaspoon cloves
¼ teaspoon salt

Preheat oven to 350 degrees. Put raisins, dates, sugar, water and shortening in a saucepan. Bring to a boil and simmer for 5 minutes. Cool. Combine dry ingredients and add to cooled boiled mixture. Bake in a greased 8 × 8-inch pan for 35 to 40 minutes. Nuts or candied fruits may be added for a holiday touch.

PINEAPPLE UPSIDE-DOWN CAKE ⊖⊕❀

   ¼ cup milk-free margarine
   ½ cup brown sugar, firmly packed
6 to 8 slices pineapple
   ⅓ cup milk-free margarine
   ⅔ cup brown sugar, firmly packed
   1 cup rye flour
   ⅔ cup rice flour
   ½ teaspoon salt
   4 teaspoons baking powder (egg-free)
   1 cup pineapple liquid (add enough water to make a cup)

Preheat oven to 375 degrees.

Melt ¼ cup margarine with ½ cup brown sugar in a 8 × 8 × 2-inch baking pan. Arrange pineapple slices in the sugar mixture. Beat ⅓ cup margarine and ⅔ cup brown sugar until creamy. Mix flours, salt and baking powder. Add flour mixture alternately with liquid to creamy mixture. Beat well after each addition. Pour batter over pineapple slices. Bake 40 to 45 minutes or until cake begins to pull away from the sides of the pan. Place plate over pan and invert. Remove pan from cake after several minutes.

APPLE PUDDING CAKE ⊖⊕❀

   ¼ cup milk-free margarine
   ½ cup sugar
   1 teaspoon vanilla
   1 cup rice flour
   ½ teaspoon cinnamon
   ½ teaspoon nutmeg
   1 teaspoon baking powder (egg-free)
   1 teaspoon baking soda
   ½ cup water
   3 cups pared and chopped apples
   ¼ cup chopped nuts

Preheat oven to 350 degrees. Grease an 8 × 8 × 2-inch baking dish. Cream together the margarine, sugar, and vanilla until fluffy.

Mix flour, cinnamon, nutmeg, baking powder and baking soda. Add flour mixture alternately with water to creamed mixture. Stir in apples and nuts. Pour into pan. Bake 40 to 45 minutes. Serve warm.

CARROT CAKE

1 teaspoon baking soda
1 teaspoon salt
2 teaspoons water
1 cup brown sugar
1¼ cups water
⅓ cup oil
⅔ cup raisins
1½ cups grated carrots
¼ teaspoon nutmeg
1½ teaspoons cinnamon
¼ teaspoon cloves
2 cups flour
2½ teaspoons baking powder (egg-free)
½ cup chopped nuts

Mix the 1 teaspoon baking soda, 1 teaspoon salt and 2 teaspoons water and set aside. Combine brown sugar, water, oil, raisins, carrots and spices in a saucepan and boil for 3 minutes. Let cool until luke-warm. Add the baking soda mixture to the brown sugar mixture. Sift together the flour and baking powder and blend in. Fold in the nuts. Bake in a greased and floured 9 × 13-inch pan at 350 degrees for 50 minutes. Frost with White Frosting (page 174) to which you have added raisins, nuts and coconut, if desired.

CARROT-PINEAPPLE CAKE [θ ϑ]

    1 cup milk-free margarine
    2 cups sugar
    4½ tablespoons oil, 4½ tablespoons water, 3 teaspoons baking
        powder (egg-free), beaten together
    2½ cups flour
    ½ teaspoon salt
    2 teaspoons cinnamon
    2 teaspoons baking soda
    2 teaspoons vanilla
    1 cup grated carrots
    1 cup drained crushed pineapple
    1 cup dried coconut
    1 cup chopped pecans
White frosting (page 174)
Pecan halves for decoration

Preheat oven to 325 degrees. Cream margarine and sugar and add the beaten mixture of oil, water and baking powder. Mix thoroughly. Sift the flour, salt, cinnamon and soda together and add to the mixture. Add the vanilla and mix well. Add the remaining ingredients. Grease and flour a 9-inch angel-food cake pan. Pour in the batter. Bake for 1 hour and 15 minutes. Let rest for 10 minutes and turn out. Frost with white frosting and decorate with pecan halves.

WHITE CAKE WITH SOY FLOUR [θ ϑ ✦]

    3 tablespoons oil
    ¾ cup sugar
    ⅔ cup soy flour
    ⅓ cup potato starch flour
    3 teaspoons baking powder (egg-free)
    ½ teaspoon salt
    ½ teaspoon mace (or spice of your choice)
    ⅓ cup water
    1 teaspoon almond flavoring (or vanilla)

Preheat oven to 275 degrees. Mix oil and sugar well. Sift dry ingredients and add to first mixture alternately with water. Add flavoring. Bake in well-greased 8-inch cake pan for 30 to 35 minutes.

PEACH AND PINEAPPLE COBBLER CAKE

2 tablespoons sugar
1 tablespoon cornstarch
½ teaspoon cinnamon
2 tablespoons lemon juice
1 1-pound can peach halves, drained (reserving liquid)
1 8¾-ounce can pineapple slices, drained (reserving liquid)
A few maraschino cherry halves
Pecans for garnish
1 cup sifted flour
2 tablespoons sugar
1½ teaspoons baking powder (egg-free)
½ teaspoon salt
⅓ cup milk-free margarine
¼ cup water

Mix 2 tablespoons sugar, cornstarch and cinnamon in a saucepan. Stir in the lemon juice and the liquid from the peaches and pineapple. Cook, stirring constantly, until thickened and smooth. Preheat oven to 400 degrees. Arrange peaches and pineapple and a few maraschino cherry halves and pecans in a 9-inch cake pan. Pour hot syrup over fruit. In a medium bowl, stir together the flour, 2 tablespoons sugar, baking powder and salt. Cut in the milk-free margarine until mixture is the consistency of cornmeal. Stir in the water and mix to form a smooth dough. Thoroughly flour hands and a sheet of wax paper. Pat dough onto the paper to form a 9-inch circle. Carefully place dough over fruit; pat smooth. Bake 25 to 30 minutes or until golden brown.
Yield: 1 9-inch cake

EGGLESS BUTTERLESS CAKE ⌷

    1 pound raisins
1½ cups sugar
    2 cups water or brewed coffee
    ½ teaspoon salt
    2 tablespoons shortening
    4 cups flour
    1 teaspoon baking soda
    1 teaspoon baking powder (egg-free)
    1 teaspoon cinnamon
    1 teaspoon nutmeg
    ½ teaspoon cloves (optional)

Boil raisins, sugar, water or coffee, salt, and shortening together for 5 minutes. Cool and then add dry ingredients which have been sifted together 3 times. Bake in two loaf pans or one tube pan at 275 degrees for 1 hour and 15 minutes to 1½ hours.

WACKY CAKE ⌷

    1 cup sugar
1½ cups flour
    3 tablespoons cocoa
    1 teaspoon baking soda
    ½ teaspoon salt
    1 tablespoon vinegar
    1 teaspoon vanilla
    6 tablespoons oil
    1 cup water

Preheat oven to 350 degrees. Sift together into an ungreased 8 × 8 × 2-inch pan the sugar, flour, cocoa, soda and salt. Make 3 holes in flour mixture. In hole one, put vinegar. In hole two, put vanilla. In hole three, put oil. Pour over this the water. Stir with fork until all the lumps are gone. Bake for 25 to 30 minutes. This makes one-half of a two-layered cake.

CHOCOLATE FUDGE UPSIDE-DOWN CAKE ⊖🎂

¾ cup granulated sugar
1 tablespoon milk-free margarine
½ cup water
1 cup flour
¼ teaspoon salt
1 teaspoon baking powder (egg-free)
1½ tablespoons cocoa
½ cup chopped walnuts
½ cup granulated sugar
½ cup brown sugar
¼ cup cocoa
1¼ cups boiling water

Preheat oven to 350 degrees. Cream together ¾ cup sugar and margarine. Add ½ cup water and stir. Sift together flour, salt, baking powder, and 1½ tablespoons cocoa and add to mixture. Stir well and put in a 9-inch greased pan. Sprinkle chopped walnuts over cake. Mix well ½ cup granulated sugar, brown sugar, and ¼ cup cocoa and spread over top. Pour boiling water over top of all. Bake for 30 minutes. Let cool in pan.

SUPER-MOIST CHOCOLATE CAKE ⊖🎂

2 cups sugar
¾ cup milk-free margarine
1½ cups boiling water
2¼ cups flour
½ cup cocoa
2 teaspoons baking soda
3 tablespoons oil, 3 tablespoons water, 2 teaspoons baking powder (egg-free), beaten together
1 teaspoon vanilla

Preheat oven to 350 degrees. Cream together the sugar and margarine in a large mixing bowl. Add the boiling water and beat. Sift dry ingredients into this mixture and mix well. Add the mixture of the 3 tablespoons oil, 3 tablespoons water and 2 teaspoons baking powder. Add the vanilla and beat for about 1 minute. Pour into greased and floured 10 × 13-inch pan. Bake 35 minutes.

FROSTINGS

CREAMY COFFEE FROSTING ⌀♁✚

⅔ cup solid vegetable shortening or milk-free margarine
6 cups sifted confectioners' sugar
6 tablespoons boiling water
1 tablespoon instant-coffee powder
2 teaspoons vanilla
¼ teaspoon salt

Thoroughly blend the shortening and 4 cups of the sifted confectioners' sugar. Beat in the boiling water, instant-coffee powder, vanilla and salt. Beat in about 2 cups confectioners' sugar, enough to make the frosting have a good consistency. Beat at high speed in an electric mixer for 1 minute.

Yield: About 3 cups, or enough to fill and frost 2 round layer cakes.

CREAMY APRICOT FROSTING ⌀♁✚

Heat a 4¾-ounce jar strained apricots with tapioca almost to a boil. Substitute the hot apricots for water and instant coffee in the recipe for Creamy Coffee Frosting above. Add 2 teaspoons lemon juice; prepare as directed.

CHOCOLATE FUDGE FROSTING

2 cups sugar
½ cup powdered unsweetened cocoa
½ cup milk-free margarine
¼ cup water
1 teaspoon vanilla

Mix all ingredients except vanilla. Bring to full rolling boil and boil 1 minute, or until mixture forms soft ball in cold water. Remove from heat, add vanilla and beat until creamy.

CARAMEL FROSTING

½ cup milk-free margarine
1 cup brown sugar, firmly packed
¼ cup water
2 cups confectioners' sugar (more if needed)

Melt margarine in a saucepan, add brown sugar. Boil over low heat 2 minutes, stirring all the time. Add water. Keep stirring until mixture boils. Remove from heat. Cool. Add sifted sugar gradually, beating well after each addition. Add pecans if desired.

NO-COOK CHOCOLATE ICING

1 box confectioners' sugar
½ cup solid vegetable shortening
8 to 10 tablespoons water
½ teaspoon salt
½ cup powdered unsweetened cocoa

Cream all of the above together

FRUIT-NUT FILLING

2/3 cup ground apricots
3/4 cups sugar
1 cup water
1/3 cup chopped nuts
1 tablespoon lemon juice
1 teaspoon grated lemon rind

Combine apricots, sugar, and water in saucepan. Simmer for 15 minutes, stirring 2 or 3 times. Cool fruit mixture; add nuts, lemon juice, and rind, stirring. Spread between sliced cake layers.

Makes enough filling for an 8- or 9-inch 3-layer cake

WHITE FROSTING

2/3 cup solid vegetable shortening
1 box confectioners' sugar
3 tablespoons water
1 teaspoon vanilla

Cream shortening until smooth and satinlike. Add powdered sugar and cream together until well blended. Add water. Beat until smooth. Chill at least 1 hour. Beat again vigorously until smooth. Add vanilla.

Makes enough to frost a 2-layer cake.

ORANGE ICING

1 pound confectioners' sugar
3 tablespoons frozen orange juice concentrate
3 tablespoons water

In medium bowl, mix confectioners' sugar with orange juice concentrate and water; blend well.

COOKIES

LEMON COOKIES

1 cup milk-free margarine
½ cup confectioners' sugar
1 teaspoon lemon or peppermint extract
2 cups flour
¼ teaspoon salt

Preheat oven to 400 degrees. Cream milk-free margarine and the sugar. Add the lemon or peppermint extract and stir. Add dry ingredients. Mix well. Shape into ½-inch balls and flatten slightly. Bake 8 to 10 minutes on an ungreased cookie sheet.
Makes 3½ dozen cookies.

NUTTY FINGERS

½ cup milk-free margarine
5 tablespoons confectioners' sugar
1 teaspoon vanilla
1 cup flour
1 cup finely chopped nuts

Preheat oven to 375 degrees. Cream margarine and add sugar and vanilla. Work in flour gradually. Add nuts. Make into rolled cookies about the size of little finger. Bake for 8 to 10 minutes or until lightly brown. When cool, roll in powdered sugar twice.

BANANA OATMEAL COOKIES

3 bananas, mashed
⅓ cup salad oil
2 cups quick-cooking uncooked oats
1½ cups chopped dates
½ cup chopped walnuts
1 teaspoon vanilla
¾ teaspoon salt

Preheat oven to 350 degrees. Mix all of the above ingredients in a large bowl. Drop by tablespoons onto an ungreased cookie sheet. Bake 20 to 25 minutes. Remove and let cool.
Makes about 30.

PUMPKIN COOKIES

½ cup milk-free margarine
1 cup sugar
1 cup puréed pumpkin
1 teaspoon vanilla
2 cups flour
1 teaspoon cinnamon
1 teaspoon baking powder (egg-free)
1 teaspoon baking soda
½ teaspoon salt
2 tablespoons water
1 cup raisins
½ cup chopped pecans

Preheat oven to 350 degrees. Cream margarine and sugar, add pumpkin and vanilla. Sift flour, cinnamon, baking powder, soda and salt together and add to the creamed mixture. Add the water and mix. Fold in raisins and nuts. Drop by teaspoonfuls onto greased cookie sheets and bake for 10 minutes.

APPLE AND SPICE COOKIES

2 cups sifted flour
1 teaspoon baking soda
½ teaspoon salt
1 teaspoon cinnamon
1 teaspoon cloves
1 teaspoon nutmeg
½ cup solid shortening
1⅓ cup brown sugar, firmly packed
⅓ cup apple juice
1 cup chopped walnuts (optional)
1 cup unpared, finely chopped cooking apples
1 cup raisins

Preheat oven to 400 degrees. Lightly grease cookie sheets. Sift together the flour, baking soda, salt and spices. In medium bowl, with electric mixer, cream shortening with brown sugar until fluffy, beat in the apple juice until smooth. Stir in flour mixture until dampened, then mix until smooth. (Mixture will be very thick.) Stir in the nuts and apples and raisins. Drop by tablespoonfuls, about 2 inches apart, onto cookie sheets. Bake 8 to 10 minutes, or until golden brown around edges and cookies feel set. Cool slightly; remove from sheets.
Makes 3 dozen.

CARROT COOKIES [⊖ 🛱]

  ½ cup boiling water
  ½ cup raisins
   1 cup brown sugar, firmly packed
  ½ cup solid shortening
 1½ tablespoons oil, 1½ tablespoons water and 1 teaspoon baking powder (egg-free), beaten together
   1 teaspoon lemon extract
  ½ cup finely shredded carrot
 1½ cups flour, sifted
   2 teaspoons baking powder (egg-free)
  ½ teaspoon salt

Preheat oven to 400 degrees. Pour boiling water over raisins; soak 5 minutes, drain. Combine brown sugar, shortening, the oil, water and baking powder mixture, and the lemon extract in a mixing bowl; beat well. Stir in carrot and drained raisins. Sift together flour, 2 teaspoons baking powder and salt; add to first mixture and blend well. Drop by teaspoonfuls on greased baking sheet. Bake for 10 to 12 minutes.
Makes 3 dozen.

OATMEAL COOKIES [⊖ 🛱 ✿]

   1 cup oat flour
   2 teaspoons baking powder (egg-free)
  ½ teaspoon baking soda
  ⅛ teaspoon salt
 1½ teaspoons cinnamon
  ⅛ teaspoon nutmeg
   1 cup oatmeal
  ½ cup chopped walnuts or pecans
  ½ cup sugar
  ¼ cup melted milk-free margarine
2 to 3 tablespoons water

Preheat oven to 350 degrees. Sift together the oat flour, baking powder, soda, salt, cinnamon and nutmeg. Combine in a bowl with the oatmeal, nuts and sugar. Blend in the melted margarine. Add water, 1 tablespoon at a time, mixing well after each addition. Form dough into small balls about the size of a plum. Place the balls on a greased cookie sheet and press with a flat-bottom glass to form circles about ⅛ inch thick. Bake for 15 minutes.

OATMEAL LACE COOKIES

½ cup milk-free margarine
½ cup brown sugar, firmly packed
½ cup granulated sugar
½ teaspoon vanilla
½ cup rice flour
½ teaspoon salt
2 teaspoons baking powder (egg-free)
¼ cup water
1½ cups quick-cooking rolled oats
¼ cup chopped nuts

Beat margarine, sugars and vanilla until creamy. Mix flour, salt and baking powder. Add flour mixture alternately with water to creamy mixture. Stir in oats and nuts; mix well. Chill overnight.

Preheat oven to 350 degrees. Grease baking sheets. Drop dough from teaspoon onto baking sheets (dough should be 1 inch in diameter); space cookies about 2 inches apart. Bake 12 to 15 minutes until lightly brown. Remove cookies from pan and finish cooling.

Makes 5 dozen.

OATMEAL COOKIES

½ cup brown sugar, firmly packed
½ cup granulated sugar
½ cup milk-free margarine
1½ tablespoons oil, 1½ tablespoons water and 1 teaspoon baking powder (egg-free), beaten together
1 teaspoon vanilla
1 tablespoon water
1 cup flour
½ teaspoon baking soda
½ teaspoon baking powder (egg-free)
½ teaspoon salt
1 cup uncooked quick-cooking rolled oats

Preheat oven to 350 degrees. Cream together the sugars and the milk-free margarine. Add the oil, water and baking powder mixture and beat well. Add the vanilla and 1 tablespoon water and beat until smooth. Sift together the flour, soda, ½ teaspoon baking powder and salt and add to the mixture. When the mixture is beaten smooth, add the oats. Beat the mixture well. Drop cookies 2 inches apart on a well-greased cookie sheet and bake until lightly brown.

Note: ¾ cup semisweet chocolate chips, raisins or pecans may be added.

OATMEAL CLUSTERS

2 cups sugar
½ cup water
½ cup milk-free margarine
Pinch of salt
1 teaspoon vanilla
½ cup peanut butter
3 cups uncooked rolled oats

Combine sugar, water, margarine and salt in a saucepan. Bring to a boil. After a full boil is reached, boil for 1 minute. Remove from heat. Add vanilla and peanut butter. Stir until smooth. Pour mixture over oatmeal and mix well. Drop on wax paper.
Makes 36 cookies.

GUM DROP COOKIES

3½ cups flour
2 teaspoons baking powder (egg-free)
1 teaspoon baking soda
1 teaspoon salt
1 cup plus 2 tablespoons oil
2 cups brown sugar, firmly packed
½ cup plus 4 tablespoons water
3 cups cut-up gum drops

Sift together the flour, baking powder, soda and salt. Mix well with remaining ingredients. Chill for 1 hour. Drop by teaspoon on a greased cookie sheet. Bake for 10 minutes at 400 degrees.
Makes 6 dozen.

CHOCOLATE CHIP COOKIES I ⌾⌗⁕

¾ cup soy flour
¼ cup potato starch flour
¼ teaspoon salt
1 teaspoon baking soda
½ cup milk-free margarine
½ cup granulated sugar
½ cup brown sugar, firmly packed
1 teaspoon vanilla
2 tablespoons oil, 4 tablespoons water and 2 teaspoons baking powder (egg-free), beaten together
1 6-ounce package chocolate chips
½ cup chopped nuts (optional)

Preheat oven to 325 degrees. Sift together the flours, salt and baking soda. Cream shortening, sugars, vanilla and the oil, water and baking powder mixture until fluffy. Add dry ingredients and mix well. Stir in chocolate chips and nuts. Drop by teaspoonfuls on a greased cookie sheet. Bake 15 to 18 minutes until lightly brown.

CHOCOLATE CHIP COOKIES II ⌾⌗

⅔ cup solid shortening
1 cup granulated sugar
½ cup brown sugar
3 tablespoons oil, 4 tablespoons water, and 2 teaspoons baking powder (egg-free), beaten together
2¼ cups flour
1 teaspoon baking soda
1 teaspoon salt
2 teaspoons vanilla
1 cup chopped nuts (optional)
1 small package semisweet chocolate chips

Preheat oven to 350 degrees. Cream shortening and sugars. Add the 3 tablespoons oil, 4 tablespoons water and 2 teaspoons baking powder mixture. Sift the dry ingredients into the mixture. Stir well. Add vanilla, nuts and chocolate chips. Mix well. The dough will be stiff. (If desired, more water may be added.) Place teaspoonfuls about 2 inches apart on a greased cookie sheet. Bake for 10 to 12 minutes. *Makes about 4 dozen.*

PEANUT BUTTER CRINKLES

    1 cup milk-free margarine
    1 cup peanut butter
    1 cup granulated sugar
    1 cup brown sugar, firmly packed
    2 teaspoons baking powder (egg-free)
    6 tablespoons water
    1 teaspoon vanilla
2½ cups flour
    1 teaspoon baking powder (egg-free)
    1 teaspoon baking soda
    1 teaspoon salt
Granulated sugar
Nuts, jam or jelly

Preheat oven to 350 degrees. In the large bowl of an electric mixer, combine the first seven ingredients and beat until light and fluffy. At low speed, add the next four ingredients. Shape into 1-inch balls and roll in sugar. Place 2 inches apart on an ungreased cookie sheet. Bake for 12 to 15 minutes or until browned. Immediately press nuts into cookies, or press with thumb and fill with jam.
Makes 6 dozen.

PEANUT BUTTER COOKIES I |ᴏ⌗✦|

> 1 cup uncooked oatmeal
> 1 cup oat flour
> 1½ teaspoons cinnamon
> ¼ teaspoon salt
> ½ teaspoon baking soda
> A little less than ½ cup sugar
> 1 cup peanut butter
> 4⅓ tablespoons melted milk-free margarine
> 3 teaspoons baking powder (egg-free)
> 2 to 4 tablespoons water

Combine all dry ingredients, except the baking powder. Cut in the peanut butter with two knives and add the melted milk-free margarine, baking powder and water. Mix thoroughly. Chill for 30 minutes. Form dough into small balls and place on a greased cookie sheet. Press with a flat-bottom glass to make circles ⅛ inch thick. Bake at 350 degrees for about 18 minutes.

PEANUT BUTTER COOKIES II |ᴏ⌗|

> 1 cup white corn syrup
> 1 cup sugar
> 1 12-ounce jar crunchy peanut butter
> 1 cup chopped pecans
> 4½ cups Special K cereal

Bring syrup and sugar to a boil. Remove from heat. Stir in peanut butter. Add pecans and cereal. Mix well. Drop from teaspoon onto waxed paper.

Makes 5 to 6 dozen.

SWEDISH COOKIES

    1 cup milk-free margarine
    2 cups sugar
    3 cups plus 2 tablespoons sifted flour
    1 teaspoon baking soda
    1 teaspoon baking powder (egg-free)
    ¼ teaspoon salt
    1 teaspoon vanilla
    1 cup shredded coconut
Nut halves
Candied cherries

Cream margarine and sugar until fluffy. Sift dry ingredients together and add to margarine. Then blend in vanilla and coconut. Chill. Form into very small balls. Place on ungreased cookie sheets. Press down with a glass that has been dipped in flour until dough is very thin. Place a nut half or piece of cherry in center of each cookie. Bake at 350 degrees until slightly brown.
Makes 100.

CHRISTMAS COOKIES

    2 cups milk-free margarine
    4 cups sifted flour
    1 teaspoon salt
    ½ teaspoon baking soda
    ¾ cup ice water
    1 teaspoon almond extract
Prune filling (see below)

Cream 1 cup margarine. Add flour and salt and mix until mixture resembles coarse crumbs. Dissolve soda in water and stir into flour mixture. Blend in almond extract. Cover dough and chill thoroughly. Roll out on a lightly floured surface in a rectangular shape about ⅛ inch thick. Spread half of dough with ½ cup soft margarine, fold over and chill in refrigerator 15 minutes. Repeat rolling, spreading and folding process. Divide dough in half and roll each portion ⅛ inch thick. Cut in 2½-inch squares and make 1-inch diagonal cuts toward center from each corner. Place 1 teaspoon of prune filling in center of each square. Bring alternate corners together in center, forming pinwheels. Bake on ungreased cookie sheets at 400 degrees for 15 minutes.

PRUNE FILLING
    1 pound cooked prunes
    ½ cup sugar
    1 teaspoon lemon juice

Remove pits from prunes and mash to a pulp. Blend in sugar and lemon juice.

DROP BROWNIES

    ½ cup milk-free margarine
    ¾ cup sugar
    1 teaspoon vanilla
    2 ounces melted unsweetened chocolate
    1¾ cup barley flour
    ½ teaspoon baking soda
    ½ teaspoon salt
    ½ cup water
Confectioners' sugar frosting (page 212), optional

Preheat oven to 400 degrees. Beat margarine, sugar, and vanilla together until creamy. Stir in the chocolate. Mix the flour, baking soda and salt together and add alternately with water to the chocolate. Drop by teaspoonfuls onto greased cookie sheets; space cookies about 2 inches apart. Bake 8 to 12 minutes. After cooling, spread cookies with frosting, if desired.

GINGERBREAD MEN

¼ cup milk-free margarine
½ cup sugar
½ cup molasses
1¼ cups rye flour
1¼ cups cornstarch
1 teaspoon baking soda
¼ teaspoon ground cloves
¾ teaspoon ground cinnamon
¼ teaspoon ginger
½ teaspoon salt
½ cup hot water
Raisins (optional)

Preheat oven to 350 degrees. Cream the milk-free margarine and sugar; add molasses. Sift the dry ingredients together and add gradually, alternating with the water. If you are using an electric mixer, it will be necessary to finish the mixing by hand. If the dough gets too gummy, add more rye flour. Roll out about ¼ inch thick on floured board or on greased cookie sheet. Cut out gingerbread men or any other pattern you wish to use. Decorate with raisins if desired. Bake for about 8 minutes, or until the cookie springs back when you press it.

When the cookies cool, you can mix together ¼ cup confectioners' sugar, a few drops of water and food coloring. Make a thick paste and use to decorate the cookies.

Makes about 18 gingerbread men

GINGERBREAD MEN II

3 cups flour
¾ teaspoon salt
1 teaspoon powdered ginger
½ teaspoon cinnamon
¼ teaspoon nutmeg
½ cup oil
½ cup molasses
Raisins or currants for garnish

Preheat oven to 350 degrees. Combine all dry ingredients. Stir in the oil and molasses. Add enough water to make a moist but rollable dough. Work as little as possible. Roll out ⅜ inch thick. Cut into desired shapes with a cookie cutter or knife. Place on greased cookie sheets. Decorate with raisins. Bake for 20 to 30 minutes or until browned.

BROWN-EYED SUSANS

1 cup milk-free margarine
3 tablespoons sugar
1 teaspoon almond extract
2 cups flour
½ teaspoon salt
Chocolate confectioners' frosting (page 189)
Almond halves

Preheat oven to 400 degrees. Cream milk-free margarine with sugar and almond extract. Blend in flour and salt. Roll level tablespoons of this mixture into balls. Place on a greased cookie sheet and flatten slightly. Bake for 10 to 12 minutes. When cool, spread ½ teaspoon of frosting on each cookie and top with an almond half in center.

CHOCOLATE CONFECTIONERS' FROSTING
1 cup confectioners' sugar
2 tablespoons cocoa
2 tablespoons hot water
½ teaspoon vanilla

Combine sugar and cocoa. Add water and vanilla and mix well.

THUMBPRINTS (PINEAPPLE)

1 cup crushed pineapple
1½ cups flour, sifted
1 teaspoon baking soda
¾ cup milk-free margarine
¾ cup brown sugar, firmly packed
¼ cup granulated sugar
1 teaspoon vanilla
1 tablespoon pineapple syrup
1½ cups corn flakes
½ cup chopped walnuts (optional)

Preheat oven to 350 degrees. Drain 1 cup of crushed pineapple and save the syrup. Sift together flour and baking soda. Cream margarine together with sugars. Add flour mixture, vanilla and pineapple syrup. Gently stir in cornflakes. Press into balls 1 inch in diameter and place on cookie sheets 2½ inches apart. Make an indentation in each with your thumb. Fill with crushed pineapple. If desired, top with chopped walnuts. Bake for 18 minutes.
Makes 2 dozen.

MAPLE COOKIES

1½ cups oat flakes
1 cup rice flour or brown rice flour
½ cup white flour
½ cup oil
1 teaspoon salt
4 tablespoons maple syrup
Water
½ to ¾ cup raisins
1 cup chopped nuts (optional)

Preheat oven to 350 degrees. Mix the oat flakes and the flours. Stir the oil into the combined flours. Add the salt, maple syrup and enough water to make a wet but not runny batter. Stir in the raisins and nuts. Drop by teaspoonfuls onto a greased cookie sheet. Press with the bottom of a glass to make the cookies flat. Bake 20 minutes.

Note: The cookies are moist and chewy if the dough is refrigerated overnight. Add more water the next day to make a wet but not runny dough. Bake.

Makes about 3 dozen cookies.

WALNUT CRESCENTS

1 cup milk-free margarine
½ cup confectioners' sugar
2 teaspoons vanilla
¼ teaspoon salt
1¾ cups flour
1 cup chopped walnuts
½ cup granulated sugar

Preheat oven to 300 degrees. Cream milk-free margarine, confectioners' sugar, vanilla and salt until fluffy. Stir in flour and walnuts until well blended. Cover and chill 30 minutes or until firm enough to handle. Break off small pieces of dough and on lightly floured surface roll with hands into finger-thick strips. Cut in 2-inch lengths; taper ends, then shape in crescents. Place 1 inch apart on an ungreased cookie sheet. Bake for 18 to 20 minutes or until firm to the touch. While warm, roll in granulated sugar. Cool and store in an airtight container in a cool place.

Makes 60.

PECAN CRESCENTS (LOW-SUGAR, CRUNCHY, CRISP)

1 cup milk-free margarine
Confectioners' sugar
1 teaspoon vanilla
¼ teaspoon salt
2¼ cups flour, sifted
¾ cup chopped pecans

Preheat oven to 400 degrees. Beat the margarine until soft, then blend in ½ cup confectioners' sugar, vanilla and salt. Add the flour gradually, blending well after each addition. Stir in the pecans. Chill the dough for 30 minutes. Mold into crescent shapes about 1 inch long and ½ inch thick. Place on ungreased baking sheets and bake for 12 to 15 minutes. While still warm, shake the cookies gently in a bag of confectioners' sugar.

Makes 4 dozen.

CHOCOLATE PEANUT BUTTER CRESCENTS (WITH DATES)

1 cup confectioners' sugar
1 cup peanut butter
1 teaspoon vanilla
1 tablespoon milk-free margarine
½ cup ground nuts
½ cup dates

Blend the above ingredients over very low heat. Shape into balls or shape of dates.

½ cup semisweet chocolate chips
1 tablespoon milk-free margarine

Melt in double boiler. Dip balls in melted mixture.

DATE CRESCENT COOKIES

1½ cups sifted flour
½ teaspoon salt
Confectioners' sugar
⅓ cup milk-free margarine
2 to 3 tablespoons cold water
1 cup dates, pitted and chopped
½ cup chopped walnuts
⅓ cup granulated sugar
½ teaspoon grated orange rind
2 tablespoons orange juice

Preheat oven to 375 degrees. Sift together flour, salt and 2 tablespoons of confectioners' sugar. Cut in the margarine until mixture resembles coarse meal. Sprinkle with water and toss lightly with fork until dough is moist enough to hold together. Form into a ball. Roll thin on floured board. Cut into 3-inch squares. Combine dates, walnuts, granulated sugar, orange rind and juice, mixing well. Put a spoonful of the date mixture on each square and bring edges together to form a triangle. Seal with a fork and curve slightly when placed on greased baking sheet. Bake for about 20 minutes. Roll in confectioners' sugar while still warm.

Makes 2 dozen.

CHECKERBOARD COOKIES

1 cup milk-free margarine
½ cup sugar
2 teaspoons vanilla
⅛ teaspoon salt
2¼ cups flour
¼ cup cocoa powder

Cream margarine, sugar, vanilla and salt until fluffy. Gradually stir in flour and mix until well blended. Roll into a ball. Divide the ball in half. With hands or sturdy spoon work cocoa into one of the dough halves until well blended. Divide each half into quarters. Shape each quarter to ½-inch-thick rope, using lightly floured hands if necessary. Place a chocolate and a white roll parallel to each other, then a white roll on top of the chocolate and a chocolate roll on the white. Press lightly to form a compact roll. Repeat with remaining dough. Wrap rolls airtight; chill several hours or overnight. Cut into 3/16-inch slices. Place ½-inch apart on a lightly greased cookie sheet. Bake at 350 degrees for 12 minutes or until white dough turns golden. Cool. Store loosely covered in cool place.

Makes about 72.

PINK-FROSTED SUGAR COOKIES

3⅔ cups sifted flour
4½ teaspoons baking powder (egg-free)
½ teaspoon salt
⅔ cup milk-free margarine
1½ cups sugar
¼ cup plus 3 teaspoons water
1 teaspoon vanilla
Pink frosting (page 194)

Measure sifted flour, add baking powder and salt and sift again. Cream milk-free margarine and add the sugar. Cream well. Add 2 to 3 teaspoons of water and beat thoroughly. Add vanilla. Add flour alternately with the ¼ cup water, mixing well after each addition. Add more water if needed. Chill overnight. Roll the dough ⅛ inch thick and cut with a 3-inch cookie cutter. Bake on a greased cookie sheet at 400 degrees for 9 minutes, or until done. Frost when cool.

PINK FROSTING

1 box confectioners' sugar
½ cup milk-free margarine
1 teaspoon vanilla
½ teaspoon salt
5 tablespoons water
Few drops of red food coloring

Beat all of the ingredients together. Add more water if needed to make a frosting that is easy to spread.

ORANGE FROSTING

Follow instructions for Pink Frosting and mix in a few drops of yellow food coloring.

SOUTHERN PECAN SHORTBREADS

Confectioners' sugar
1 cup milk-free margarine
1 teaspoon vanilla
1 cup finely chopped pecans
2 cups flour, sifted

Preheat oven to 325 degrees. Mix ⅔ cup confectioners' sugar with rest of ingredients and blend thoroughly with hands. Warmth of hands is necessary for blending. Roll out ⅜ inches thick and cut with 1¼-inch cutter into desired shapes. Place on an ungreased baking sheet and bake until barely starting to brown. Overbrowning spoils flavor. While still hot, roll in powdered sugar.

JACK O'LANTERN COOKIES

4½ cups flour
½ cup wheat germ
½ teaspoon salt
¼ teaspoon baking soda
2 teaspoons cinnamon
1 teaspoon ground cloves
1 teaspoon ginger
½ cup milk-free margarine
1 cup sugar
1 cup molasses
1 cup canned pumpkin
Orange Frosting (page 194)
Nuts and candies for decorating

Sift together the flour, wheat germ, salt, baking soda, cinnamon, cloves and ginger. In a large bowl, cream milk-free margarine and sugar until light and fluffy. Blend in molasses and pumpkin. Gradually add the flour mixture, blending at low speed in an electric mixer

(continued)

until well mixed. Divide the dough into 4 equal parts: refrigerate, wrapped in waxed paper, at least 30 minutes.

Preheat oven to 375 degrees. On a floured board, knead each piece of dough into a smooth ball. (Keep remaining dough in the refrigerator until ready to use.) With a floured rolling pin, roll out each ball to ¼-inch thickness. Cut with pumpkin cookie cutter or cut around a cardboard cutout of your own design. Place cookies on a greased cookie sheet. Bake for 8 to 10 minutes. Cool. When luke-warm, carefully press wooden skewer into bottom of cookie to form a cookie "pop." Frost with Orange Frosting. Decorate.

CORNMEAL COOKIES

⅓ cup milk-free margarine
1 cup packed brown sugar
1 tablespoon oil
2 tablespoons water
1 teaspoon baking powder (egg-free)
3 tablespoons fruit juice
2 cups cornmeal
1 teaspoon vanilla

Preheat oven to 375 degrees. Cream margarine and sugar. Add 1 tablespoon oil, 2 tablespoons water and 1 teaspoon baking powder and mix well. Add remaining ingredients. Drop on a greased cookie sheet with teaspoon and bake for 15 minutes.

Makes 5 dozen.

RICE OR BARLEY COOKIES

¼ cup honey
⅓ cup oil
½ cup sugar
1 cup rice flour or barley flour
½ teaspoon baking powder (egg-free)
¼ teaspoon baking soda
¼ teaspoon salt
½ teaspoon vanilla

Preheat oven to 375 degrees. Mix all ingredients together thoroughly. Drop by teaspoonfuls onto greased cookie sheets. Bake for about 10 to 15 minutes.

CINNAMON BUTTER COOKIES

½ cup milk-free margarine
1 cup brown sugar
¼ cup cold water
2 cups flour
1 teaspoon baking soda
½ teaspoon salt
½ teaspoon cinnamon

Mix milk-free margarine and sugar thoroughly. Stir in cold water. Sift together and blend in dry ingredients. Mix thoroughly with hands and shape into long roll. Chill until stiff (overnight is best).

Preheat oven to 400 degrees. Cut in ¼-inch slices. Bake 6 to 8 minutes on an ungreased cookie sheet.

Makes 4 dozen cookies

BUTTER COOKIES

1 cup milk-free margarine
1 cup sifted confectioners' sugar
1 teaspoon vanilla
2¼ cups flour
¼ teaspoon salt
Colored sugar, ground coconut, ground nuts

Mix first three ingredients thoroughly. Stir in flour and salt. Mix with hands. Shape into 2 rolls, about 2 inches in diameter. Roll one roll in colored sugar and the other in ground coconut or ground nuts. Chill several hours.

Preheat oven to 400 degrees. Cut dough into slices about ⅛ inch thick. Bake 8 to 10 minutes on an ungreased cookie sheet.

Makes 4½ dozen cookies.

PECAN DROPS

1 cup pecans
½ cup milk-free margarine
½ cup plus 2 tablespoons shortening
1 cup confectioners' sugar
2½ cups sifted flour
2 teaspoons vanilla

Preheat oven to 325 degrees and chop pecans coarsely. Cream margarine and shortening together until smooth. Then beat in the confectioners' sugar gradually. Stir in the flour thoroughly and add vanilla and pecans. Mix well and drop by teaspoon onto an ungreased cookie sheet. Bake 15 to 20 minutes or until light golden brown.

Makes 4 dozen

PEANUT BUTTER BARS

4 cups puffed rice cereal
¼ cup milk-free margarine or solid vegetable shortening
⅓ cup peanut butter
32 large marshmallows
½ teaspoon vanilla

Heat puffed rice in shallow pan at 350 degrees for 10 minutes. Pour into greased large bowl. Melt margarine or shortening, peanut butter and marshmallows over low heat (may use double boiler). Stir until smooth. Add vanilla. Pour marshmallow mixture over puffed rice, stirring until evenly coated. Press into greased 11 × 7-inch baking pan. When cool, cut into bars.
Makes 2 dozen bars

MOLASSES DROP COOKIES

2 cups sifted rye flour
2 teaspoons baking powder (egg-free)
½ teaspoon salt
¼ teaspoon ginger
½ teaspoon nutmeg
½ cup solid shortening
½ cup sugar
½ cup molasses
¼ cup sweetened applesauce
½ cup raisins or ¼ cup chopped nuts

Preheat oven to 400 degrees. Lightly grease cookie sheets. Sift together the flour, baking powder, salt, ginger and nutmeg. In a medium bowl, cream together the shortening and sugar until light and fluffy; beat in the molasses. Add ⅓ rye-flour mixture to shortening; beat until smooth. Add applesauce and beat until smooth. Add another third of the rye-flour mixture and beat until smooth. Add the remaining rye-flour mixture and beat until smooth. Beat in the raisins or the nuts, if desired. Drop by tablespoonfuls, 2 inches apart, onto the greased cookie sheets. Bake 7 minutes, or until cookies feel set.

Makes 3 to 4 dozen

FRUITY BARS

1¾ cups flour
½ teaspoon baking soda
¾ cup milk-free margarine
1 cup brown sugar, firmly packed
1½ cups quick oats
1 cup strawberry or raspberry jam (one 12-ounce jar)

Preheat oven to 400 degrees. Stir together the flour and soda; set aside. Cream margarine and sugar until light and fluffy. Stir in flour mixture until well blended. Blend in oats. Dough will be crumbly. Press half the dough into greased 13 × 9-inch pan. Spread with jam. Crumble remaining dough over top; pat lightly to cover. Bake for 20 to 25 minutes or until lightly browned. While warm, cut into bars.

Makes 30

OATMEAL BARS

½ cup melted and cooled milk-free margarine
2 cups quick-cooking oats
½ cup light brown sugar, firmly packed
¼ cup white corn syrup
½ teaspoon salt
1½ teaspoons vanilla

Preheat oven to 450 degrees. Blend all the ingredients well and pack into greased 9-inch square pan. The pan should be lined with aluminum foil because this recipe will be sticky. Bake for 12 minutes. Cool and cut into bars.

TOFFEE BARS

 2 cups quick-cooking rolled oats
 ½ cup brown sugar, firmly packed
 Pinch of salt
 ¼ cup light corn syrup
 ⅓ cup melted milk-free margarine
 ½ teaspoon vanilla
 1 package semisweet chocolate chips
 ⅓ cup nut meats

Preheat oven to 350 degrees. Combine rolled oats, brown sugar and salt. Add syrup, margarine and vanilla. Mix. Pat into 13 × 9-inch pan. Bake for 10 minutes. Remove from oven, sprinkle on chocolate chips, return to oven just long enough to soften chips. Remove from oven, spread chips with spatula and sprinkle with nut meats. Cut and remove from pan at once.
Makes 12

APRICOT DATE BARS

 ¾ cup oil
 1 cup brown sugar, firmly packed
 2 cups flour
 1 teaspoon baking soda
 2 cups quick-cooking oats
 1 teaspoon vanilla
 Date-Apricot Filling (page 202)

Preheat oven to 350 degrees. Blend oil and sugar. Add sifted flour, soda, oats and vanilla. Work with hands into a dough. Press half of this mixture on bottom of greased pan. Spread filling over surface. Top with remaining mixture. Bake for 30 minutes.

(continued)

DATE-APRICOT FILLING
 ½ pound dates (1 cup)
 1 No. 2½ can apricots or 3½ cups stewed dried apricots
 ½ cup brown sugar, firmly packed
 2 tablespoons cold water

Cut dates into small pieces. Drain apricots. Add sugar and water and boil till thick, about 3 minutes. Cool slightly.

APPLE OATMEAL BARS

 1 cup flour
 ½ teaspoon salt
 ½ teaspoon baking soda
 ½ cup plus 2 tablespoons milk-free margarine
 ½ cup brown sugar, firmly packed
 1½ cups uncooked rolled oats
 2 to 3 apples, cored and peeled
 ½ cup sugar mixed with 2 teaspoons cinnamon

Preheat oven to 350 degrees. Sift flour, salt, and soda together. Work in ½ cup margarine. Blend with brown sugar and oatmeal. Spread ½ to ⅔ of the mixture on bottom of ungreased 9 × 9-inch baking pan. Press to form a crust. Slice apples on crust. Sprinkle with sugar and cinnamon mixture. Dot with 2 tablespoons margarine. Spread rest of crumbled mixture over apples. Bake for 40 to 45 minutes. Cut into squares and serve warm. Or cut into bars and serve cold.

EASY CHEWY BARS

 1 package of semisweet chocolate chips (12 ounces)
 1 cup peanut butter
 2 cups miniature marshmallows
 1 cup salted peanuts (more if desired)

Mix chocolate and peanut butter in top of a double boiler and heat until chips have melted. In an oiled 9 × 12-inch pan, spread marshmallows; add peanuts. Pour first mixture over marshmallows and peanuts. Refrigerate. Cut into squares.

SAND BARS

1 cup milk-free margarine
6 tablespoons granulated sugar
3 cups flour
1 cup chopped nuts
2 teaspoons vanilla
Small amount of tart jelly
100 pecan halves
½ cup confectioners' sugar

Preheat oven to 300 degrees. Cream margarine and granulated sugar, add flour gradually. Then blend in chopped nuts and vanilla. This makes a firm dough. Pinch off small amounts and roll into balls. Push thumb into balls to make a deep dent. Fill with tart jelly. Top with pecan. Place about 2 inches apart on oiled baking sheet and bake for 30 minutes. When cool roll in confectioners' sugar.
Makes 100.

SCRABBLE SQUARES

2 cups semisweet chocolate chips
2 tablespoons solid shortening
3 cups tiny marshmallows
2 cups chow mein noodles

Melt chocolate chips and shortening. Mix tiny marshmallows and chow mein noodles. Chill in 9-inch pan. Cut into squares.

PECAN BARS

2 cups milk-free margarine
4½ cups confectioners' sugar
4 cups chopped pecans
4 cups flour
2 teaspoons vanilla
2 tablespoons ice water

Preheat oven to 350 degrees. Cream margarine thoroughly, add 8 tablespoons sugar and continue creaming until all is blended. Mix nuts and flour and add to creamed mixture gradually until well blended. Add vanilla and ice water and mix. Roll pieces of dough with palm of hand into 1-inch rolls of half-moon designs. Bake on ungreased cookie sheet for 35 minutes until golden brown. Sift powdered sugar generously over rolls and place in cookie jar to preserve.

PEANUT CRUNCH BARS

1 cup sugar
1 cup corn syrup
1½ cups crunchy peanut butter
5 cups cereal, such as Special K cereal

Combine sugar and corn syrup in a saucepan and bring to a boil, do not cook. Add peanut butter. Add cereal. Put in 8 × 14-in pan and pack down. Cool and frost. Cut into bars.

FROSTING
1 cup sugar
¼ cup cocoa
¼ cup water or nondairy creamer
¼ cup milk-free margarine

Boil 1 minute; beat well.
Makes 24.

RAISIN MUMBLES

2½ cups raisins
½ cup granulated sugar
2 tablespoons cornstarch
¾ cup water
3 tablespoons lemon juice
¾ cup milk-free margarine, softened
1 cup brown sugar, firmly packed
1¾ cups sifted flour
½ teaspoon salt
½ teaspoon baking soda
1½ cups rolled oats

Cook raisins, granulated sugar, cornstarch, water and lemon juice together, stirring constantly over low heat until thick. Cool.

Preheat oven to 400 degrees. Cream margarine and brown sugar. Add dry ingredients, then oats. Press half of mixture into a 13 × 9-inch pan. Spread with the cooled filling. Pat on remaining crumbs. Smooth with back of spoon. Bake for 20 to 30 minutes. Cool before cutting, otherwise the cookies will fall apart.

Makes 6 dozen

CRUNCHY APPLESAUCE SQUARES

CRUST
½ cup milk-free margarine
¾ cup brown sugar, firmly packed
¾ cup flour
1 cup quick oats
½ teaspoon salt

Preheat oven to 350 degrees. Cream together margarine and brown sugar. Add flour, oats and salt. Cut together until crumbly. Press one half mixture into an 8 × 8 × 1½-inch greased pan. Bake for 20 minutes.

(continued)

FILLING

    1½ cups canned applesauce
    2 tablespoons flour
    ¼ cup brown sugar
    ½ teaspoon lemon rind
    1 tablespoon lemon juice

Pour applesauce into saucepan. Boil rapidly for 5 minutes, stirring constantly. Combine flour with brown sugar. Add to hot applesauce. Cook about 5 minutes or until thickened. Remove from heat, add lemon rind and juice. Cool.

TO ASSEMBLE

    ½ cup chopped walnuts
    ½ teaspoon nutmeg
    Remaining crust mixture

Spread filling evenly over baked crust. Add nuts and nutmeg to remaining crust mixture; blend well. Sprinkle over applesauce mixture. Bake at 375 degrees for 40 minutes. Cut when cool.
Makes 9 servings.

HONEY SQUARES

    ¾ cup oil
    1 cup sugar
    ¼ cup honey
    2 cups flour
    1 teaspoon baking soda
    1 teaspoon cinnamon
    ½ teaspoon salt
    1 tablespoon oil, 2 tablespoons water and 1 teaspoon baking powder (egg-free), beaten together
Confectioners' Sugar Icing (page 212)

Preheat oven to 350 degrees. Mix the ¾ cup oil, sugar and honey together. Sift together the flour, baking soda, cinnamon and salt and add to the honey mixture. Add the mixture of oil, water and baking powder and beat well. Press into greased and floured pan. Bake for 18 minutes. Slice and glaze immediately with Confectioners' Sugar Icing.

SPICED SQUARES

    1 cup brown sugar, firmly packed
1¼ cups water
    ⅓ cup solid shortening
    1 cup raisins
    ⅔ cup yellow cornmeal
    ⅔ cup sifted rye flour
    ⅔ cup rice flour
1½ teaspoons double-acting baking powder (egg-free)
    ½ teaspoon salt
1¼ teaspoons nutmeg
    1 teaspoon cinnamon

In a medium saucepan, simmer the brown sugar, water, shortening and raisins for 3 minutes; cool to room temperature. Sift together the cornmeal, rye flour and rice flour. Stir in the remaining ingredients. Preheat oven to 350 degrees. Grease an 8 × 8 × 2-inch baking pan. Thoroughly mix dry ingredients into sugar mixture. Spread in pan; bake for 45 minutes or until browned.

Makes 16 squares

RAISIN SQUARES $\boxed{\;\theta\,\beta\;}$

    2 cups raisins
1½ cups water
    2 tablespoons milk-free margarine
    ¼ teaspoon salt
    ½ cup honey
    1 teaspoon allspice
    1 teaspoon cinnamon
    2 cups chopped nuts
    2 cups flour

Place the raisins, water, milk-free margarine and salt in a saucepan and bring to a boil; simmer for 3 minutes. Add the honey while this mixture is still hot. Cool. Preheat oven to 350 degrees. Mix the spices, nuts and flour and add to the raisin mixture. Stir well. Pour into greased and floured 8 × 8-inch cake pan. Bake 45 minutes to 1 hour.

Cool. Cut. Chewy squares are best the second or third day.

CRISPY MARSHMALLOW TREATS $\boxed{\;\theta\,\beta\,\ast\;}$

    ¼ cup milk-free margarine
    1 package (10 ounces, or about 40) large marshmallows or 4
      cups miniature marshmallows
    5 cups rice cereal

Melt margarine in a large saucepan over low heat. Add marshmallows and stir until melted and well blended. Remove from heat. Add cereal. Stir until well coated. Press mixture evenly into greased 13 × 9 × 2-inch pan. Cool completely. Cut into squares.

CHOCOLATE CRISPIES 🖉🛏🌸

    1 6-ounce package semisweet chocolate pieces
    ½ cup chunky-style or creamy-style peanut butter
    1 teaspoon vanilla
    3 cups crisp rice cereal

Lightly grease a 9 × 9 × 2-inch baking dish.

In top of double boiler, over hot water, melt together the chocolate pieces and peanut butter; beat until smooth; beat in vanilla.

Add rice cereal; mix thoroughly. Turn into baking dish; smooth surface. Cool until set. Cut into thirty-six 1½-inch squares.

ALMOND COOKIES 🖉🛏🌸

    1 cup rice flour or potato-starch flour
    ½ cup brown sugar, firmly packed
    2 cups finely ground blanched almonds
    ½ cup melted milk-free margarine
    1 tablespoon ice water

Preheat oven to 350 degrees. Grease cookie sheets. Stir together the flour and brown sugar. In a medium bowl, stir together the sugar-flour mixture and the almonds. Add margarine. Beat until mixed. Add the water and beat until mixture just begins to stick together and form a ball. Shape dough into balls the size of small walnuts; place 2 inches apart on the cookie sheets. With a flat-bottomed glass, press cookies into circles 2½ inches in diameter. Bake 10 minutes or until cookies are golden.

Makes about 2½ dozen

NUT GEMS

1 cup milk-free margarine
Confectioners' sugar
2 cups sifted flour
1 cup chopped nuts
2 tablespoons water
1 teaspoon rum flavoring or vanilla extract

Preheat oven to 350 degrees. Cream margarine, add 4 table-spoons sugar gradually, cream until smooth. Blend in flour. Stir in nuts, water, and flavoring. Mix well. Shape into 1-inch balls. Bake on ungreased baking sheet for 20 minutes or until golden brown. While still warm, roll in confectioners' sugar.

PUFFED RICE CANDY BALLS

6 cups puffed rice cereal
¾ cup light corn syrup
¼ cup light molasses
½ teaspoon salt
1 teaspoon vinegar
2 tablespoons milk-free margarine
1 teaspoon vanilla

Heat puffed rice in shallow baking pan at 350 degrees for 10 minutes. Pour into greased large bowl. Combine syrup, molasses, salt and vinegar in saucepan. Cook over medium heat, stirring occasion-ally, to hard-ball stage (255 degrees) or until syrup dropped into cold water forms a hard ball. Remove from heat; stir in margarine and vanilla. Pour over puffed rice, stirring until evenly coated. With greased hands, shape to form balls.
Makes 12 balls.

PECAN BUTTER BALLS

2 cups flour
¼ cup granulated sugar
½ teaspoon salt
1 cup milk-free margarine, softened
2 teaspoons vanilla
2 cups finely chopped pecans
3 tablespoons confectioners' sugar

Preheat oven to 325 degrees. Stir together flour, sugar and salt; add milk-free margarine and vanilla, blending with a wooden spoon until soft, smooth dough is formed. Add pecans; mix well. Shape in to 1-inch balls. Bake on an ungreased cookie sheet for 25 minutes or until firm and lightly browned on bottom. Remove to racks set over waxed paper. While still warm, sift confectioners' sugar over tops. Cool completely; store in an airtight container and place in a cool place.
Makes 48.

WEDDING COOKIES

1 cup milk-free margarine
Confectioners' sugar
1 teaspoon vanilla
¼ teaspoon salt
2 cups flour

Cream the milk-free margarine with ½ cup confectioners' sugar, vanilla and salt until fluffy. Stir in flour until well blended. Chill 30 minutes or until firm enough to handle. Shape into 1-inch balls. Place 1 inch apart on an ungreased cookie sheet; bake at 375 degrees for 12 to 15 minutes, or until lightly golden. Remove and, while still warm, dust heavily with confectioners' sugar; cool. Store airtight in cool, dry place. Before serving, dust cookies with additional confectioners' sugar.
Makes 48.

CHERRY BONBONS

½ cup milk-free margarine
¼ cup confectioners' sugar
½ teaspoon vanilla
1 cup flour
¼ cup finely chopped nuts
½ pound (1½ cups) red candied cherries
Confectioners' Sugar Frosting (see below)
Sliced red candied cherries

Cream margarine, sugar and vanilla until light. Stir in flour and nuts until well blended. Cover and chill 30 minutes or until firm enough to handle. On lightly floured surface shape in to 1-inch-thick rolls. Cut into ½-inch slices. Turn cut side up; place cherry in center of each slice. With lightly floured hands shape balls, covering cherry completely with dough. Place 1 inch apart on an ungreased cookie sheet; chill 15 minutes. Bake at 350 degrees for 15 to 20 minutes or until lightly browned. Remove and cool. To frost, set cookies on a rack over waxed paper. Spoon frosting over cookies, allowing it to run down sides. (Scrape up dripping frosting and reuse.) Decorate with sliced cherries. Store in an airtight container in a cool place. *Makes 24.*

CONFECTIONERS' SUGAR FROSTING

1 cup confectioners' sugar
1 to 1½ tablespoons water
¼ teaspoon vanilla

Mix all of the ingredients above to the consistency desired.

PINEAPPLE—GRAHAM CRACKER PUDDING

1 cup milk-free margarine
1 cup sugar
1 small can crushed pineapple, undrained
2 packages graham crackers

Melt the cup of milk-free margarine and add the sugar and pineapple. Crush 1 package of graham crackers, add to the mixture. Place whole graham crackers on the bottom of a casserole, then the pineapple mixture on top, then a layer of the whole graham crackers, then the pineapple mixture, etc., until all of the mixture is used. Refrigerate.

COCONUT BALLS

1 cup milk-free margarine, softened
¼ cup sifted confectioners' sugar
2 teaspoons vanilla
1 tablespoon water
2 cups sifted flour
1 cup chopped pecans
Frosting (see page 214)
18 ounces (3 cups) shredded coconut, cut fine
Assorted food colorings (pink, yellow, green)

Preheat oven to 300 degrees. Thoroughly cream margarine, sugar, and vanilla. Stir in water. Add flour and mix well. Stir in nuts. Roll into 1-inch balls. Bake on ungreased cookie sheet for 20 minutes, or until delicately browned. Cool thoroughly before removing from pan. Tint coconut: Place coconut in jar, add a few drops coloring, cover, shake until color is uniform. Dip balls in frosting and roll in tinted coconut.

(continued)

FROSTING

    4 cups sifted confectioners' sugar
    ½ cup water

Gradually add water to sugar, blending until smooth.

HONEY SUNDIES

    1 cup solid shortening
    2 cups sifted flour
    ¼ cup honey
    ½ teaspoon vanilla or almond extract
    ½ teaspoon salt
    2 cups chopped pecans
Confectioners' sugar

Preheat oven to 300 degrees. Cream shortening. Add other ingredients except sugar. Roll into small balls. Bake for 30 minutes. Roll in powdered sugar while hot, and again when cold.

BON BONS

    ¼ cup lemon juice
    ¼ cup orange juice
    1 tablespoon grated lemon or orange rind
    3 cups finely crushed graham cracker crumbs
    2 tablespoons cocoa
    1 cup powdered sugar
    1 cup finely chopped nuts
Granulated sugar

Mix the first 7 ingredients together in a bowl. Blend well and shape into balls. Roll in granulated sugar.

BUTTER BON BONS

1 cup milk-free margarine
½ cup sifted confectioners' sugar
1 teaspoon vanilla
2 cups sifted flour
½ teaspoon salt
Flaked or shredded coconut
1 cup oats (quick-cooking or old-fashioned kind), uncooked
½ cup semisweet chocolate chips

Preheat oven to 325 degrees. Beat together the margarine, sugar, and vanilla until creamy. Sift together flour and salt, blend well into the margarine mixture. Stir in ½ cup coconut and rolled oats. Shape dough into balls (1 tablespoon each). Bake on an ungreased cookie sheet in preheated oven for about 25 minutes. Cool. Melt semisweet chocolate pieces over hot water. Swirl chocolate on cookies; sprinkle with coconut.

PECAN STICKS

1 cup milk-free margarine
⅔ cup sugar
1 teaspoon water
1 teaspoon vanilla or almond extract
2¼ cups flour
½ cup chopped nuts

Preheat oven to 350 degrees. Cream margarine. Add sugar and cream well. Add water and vanilla. Gradually add flour until mixed into a stiff dough. Blend in chopped nuts. Chill until dough becomes firm. Roll pieces of dough in palm of hand into shape of small cocoons. Place on ungreased cookie sheet. Bake 8 to 10 minutes until lightly browned.
Makes 75 cookies.

FRUIT ROLLS ⌀∄✚

1 cup pressed figs
1 cup pitted dates
1 cup seedless raisins
½ cup candied orange peel
½ cup nuts
2 tablespoons lemon juice
Powdered sugar

Mix fruit and nuts and put through meat chopper, using medium knife. Work in lemon juice and shape into rolls or small balls. Slice rolls and roll in sugar or roll balls same way.

LACY ALMOND ROLLS ⌀∄✚

⅔ cup finely ground blanched almonds
½ cup milk-free margarine
½ cup granulated sugar
2 tablespoons water
1 tablespoon rice flour
Confectioners' sugar

Preheat oven to 350 degrees. Grease and flour (using rice flour) cookie sheets. In a large skillet, thoroughly stir together the almonds, margarine, granulated sugar, water and flour. Stir over low heat until margarine is melted and mixture boils and is a liquid. Drop batter by teaspoonfuls on the prepared cookie sheets, 3 inches apart. Bake 5 to 6 minutes or until golden brown. Let cool slightly, then remove cookies one at a time. Quickly roll up around handle of wooden spoon; cool. (If cookie becomes too hard to roll, warm in oven a minute or so, then roll.) Dust lightly with sifted confectioners' sugar.
Makes about 2½ dozen.

Note: Add more water if necessary to keep the almond mixture thin and runny.

LACY ENGLISH JUMBOS

1 6-ounce package of semisweet chocolate chips
¾ cup solid shortening
¾ cup sugar
⅛ teaspoon salt
¼ teaspoon ginger
½ cup light corn syrup
1½ cups sifted flour

Preheat oven to 350 degrees. Combine chocolate bits, shortening, sugar, salt, and ginger. Melt over hot water. Remove from heat. Stir in corn syrup and sifted flour. Drop by teaspoonfuls 3 inches apart on well-greased cookie sheet. Bake for 10 minutes. Cool slightly, approximately 1 minute. Remove from cookie sheet and roll at once, top side down, over handle of wooden spoon, or use finger to form a cane. Press to seal edges. If cookies should stick to the sheet, return to oven for a minute. Then proceed as directed.

PIES

FRESH FRUIT PIE |♂⊕✦|

2 cups cut-up fresh fruit
½ cup fruit juice (any kind)
2½ tablespoons tapioca
⅛ teaspoon salt
¾ to 1 cup sugar
½ teaspoon vanilla
1 unbaked 9-inch pie shell (made to fit allowed diet) (see pages 223–225)

Preheat oven to 425 degrees. Combine first 6 ingredients in a bowl. Let stand for 15 minutes. Pour into pie shell. Bake for 35 to 45 minutes.

BLUEBERRY PIE |♂⊕✦|

1 cup sugar
2 tablespoons cornstarch
1 cup boiling water
2 cups fresh or frozen blueberries
¼ teaspoon cinnamon
⅛ teaspoon cloves
¼ teaspoon salt
2 tablespoons lemon juice
Baked 9-inch pie shell (made to fit allowed diet) (see pages 223–225)
Nondairy topping

Sift together the sugar and cornstarch. Put into a saucepan. Add the boiling water and stir until thoroughly mixed. Add 1 cup blueberries and boil until blueberries burst and mixture thickens. Add cinnamon, cloves, salt and lemon juice. Put remaining cup of berries in bottom of pastry shell and immediately pour the cooked mixture over them. Allow to cool. Serve with nondairy topping.

DELUXE CHERRY PIE

2 cups pitted cherries, drained (frozen or canned)
⅓ cup cherry juice
⅛ teaspoon almond extract
⅓ cup granulated sugar
⅓ cup brown sugar
3 tablespoons quick-cooking tapioca
Pastry for a double-pie crust (made to fit allowed diet) (see pages 223–225)
1 tablespoon milk-free margarine

Combine cherries, juice, almond extract, sugars, and tapioca; let stand 15 minutes. Pour into pastry-lined 8-inch pie pan, dot with margarine. Adjust top crust and flute edge. Bake at 450 degrees for 10 minutes, then at 350 degrees for 30 minutes.

DEEP-DISH FRESH PEACH PIE

6 fresh peaches, sliced
1 cup plus 1 tablespoon sugar
¼ teaspoon salt
1½ tablespoons quick-cooking tapioca
Milk-free margarine
Pastry strips for cover (made to suit allowed diet) (see pastry recipes pages 223–225)

Combine peaches, 1 cup sugar, salt and tapioca. Turn into a casserole and dot with 2 tablespoons margarine. Cover with pastry strips rolled to ⅛ inch thick, cutting gashes in pastry if full topping is used. Sprinkle top with remaining sugar and dot with margarine. Bake at 425 degrees for 30 to 40 minutes.

FRUIT GLAZE PIE [θ ♗ ♦]

> 1 baked pastry shell (using ingredients that are tolerated) (see pages 223–225)
> 2 cups fresh berries or peaches
> 1 cup water
> 1 cup sugar
> 3 tablespoons cornstarch
> 1 tablespoon lemon juice
> Nondairy topping

Half fill a baked pastry shell with 1 cup fresh strawberries, raspberries or peaches. Simmer 1 cup fruit and water for 5 minutes. Thicken the mixture with cornstarch and sugar which have been mixed together and cook until thick and clear. Add lemon juice and cool. Pour the cooked mixture over the fresh fruit. Chill and top with a nondairy topping.

STRAWBERRY GLAZE PIE [θ ♗ ♦]

OATMEAL PIE CRUST
> 1⅓ cups quick-cooking or old-fashioned oats, uncooked
> ⅓ cup brown sugar, firmly packed
> ⅓ cup milk-free margarine

FILLING
> 3 pints fresh strawberries, hulled and washed
> 1 cup sugar
> 1 envelope (1 tablespoon) unflavored gelatin
> Dash of salt
> ½ cup water
> 1 tablespoon lemon juice

For crust: Preheat oven to 350 degrees. Combine oats and brown sugar. Add melted margarine; mix until crumbly. Press firmly onto bottom and sides of a 9-inch pie plate. Place a 8-inch pie plate on top of the crust mixture; press down. Bake in preheated oven for about 8 minutes. Remove 8-inch pie plate and cool.

For filling: Crush and strain enough strawberries to make 1 cup of liquid. Combine sugar, gelatin and salt in a medium saucepan. Add strawberry liquid, water and lemon juice. Cook over medium heat, stirring constantly, about 3 minutes or until sugar dissolves. Cool. Add strawberries. Chill until partially thickened. Pour into pie shell. Refrigerate.

PUMPKIN PIE

 2 cups canned pumpkin
 2/3 cup brown sugar, firmly packed
 1½ cups water
 6 tablespoons instant tapioca
 1 teaspoon pumpkin pie spice
 ½ teaspoon salt
 1 unbaked pie shell (baked to suit your allergy limitations) (see pages 223–225)

TOPPING
 ¼ cup brown sugar
 ¼ cup shredded coconut
 ¼ cup chopped pecans

Combine first 6 ingredients in a saucepan. Cook over low heat until mixture thickens and the tapioca is clear. Pour into pie shell. Bake for 30 minutes at 375 degrees. Combine ingredients for topping and sprinkle over the top of the pie. Bake 5 minutes more. Let cool and set before serving.

LIGHT AND FLUFFY PIE ⟨ᵉ⟩

1 (3-ounce) package gelatin, your choice of flavor
⅔ cup boiling water
2 cups ice cubes
8 ounces nondairy whipped topping
1 cup fresh fruit; or 1 8¾-ounce can apricots, sliced peaches,
    drained and diced, or fruit cocktail, drained; or 1 (8¼-ounce)
    can crushed pineapple, drained
Baked graham cracker pie crust (page 225)

Dissolve gelatin completely in boiling water, stirring about 3 minutes. Add ice cubes and stir until gelatin is thickened, about 2 to 3 minutes. Remove any unmelted ice. Then blend in the nondairy whipped topping and whip until smooth. Fold in fruit. Chill, if necessary, until mixture will mound. Spoon into graham-cracker pie crust. Chill 2 hours.

ROYAL HAWAIIAN BANANA PIE ⟨ᵉ⟩

4 cups sliced firm ripe bananas (5 to 6 medium)
½ cup pineapple juice
1 9-inch double pie crust (made to fit allowed diet) (see pages
    223–225)
½ cup sugar
1 teaspoon cinnamon
2 tablespoons milk-free margarine

Slice bananas. Cover with pineapple juice. Toss gently until slices are coated. Let set 30 minutes. Drain. Place bananas in uncooked shell. Mix sugar and cinnamon. Sift over top of bananas. Dot with margarine. Put on top crust, seal edges. Vent top with 2 or 3 slashes near center. Bake at 400 degrees for about 30 minutes or until the crust is golden brown.

FLAKY PIE CRUST

2 cups flour
1 teaspoon salt
¾ cup solid shortening
5 to 6 tablespoons cold water

TWO-CRUST PIE

In a medium bowl, with a fork, mix flour with salt. With a pastry blender or two knives used scissor-fashion, cut in shortening until the mixture resembles coarse crumbs. Sprinkle 5 to 6 tablespoons of cold water, a tablespoon at a time, into mixture, mixing lightly with a fork after each addition until pastry is just moist enough to hold together. Shape pastry into a ball; divide into two pieces, one slightly larger; shape each into a ball.

For bottom crust: On a lightly floured surface, with a floured rolling pin, roll larger ball into a circle ⅛ inch thick and 2 inches larger all around than pie pan. Fold pastry into fourths and place in pan with point in center. Unfold and ease into pan, lifting toward center so it won't stretch or shrink during baking. With scissors, trim edge, leaving ½-inch overhang.

For top crust: See the pie recipe you are using.

UNBAKED SINGLE PIE CRUST

Prepare as in Flaky Pie Crust but use only 1 cup of flour, ½ teaspoon salt, ¼ cup plus 2 tablespoons shortening, 2 to 3 tablespoons water. Shape pastry into one ball. Roll and line pan as for bottom pie crust, leaving 1-inch overhang. Fold overhang under; pinch to form high edge; flute.

(continued)

BAKED PIE CRUST

Preheat oven to 425 degrees. Prick crust in many places to prevent puffing. Bake 15 minutes or until golden brown; check after first 5 minutes; if puffed, prick again.

OATMEAL PIE CRUST

See page 220.

COCONUT PIE CRUST

2 cups flaked coconut
¼ cup milk-free margarine

Lightly brown coconut in margarine. Press mixture into bottom and sides of an oiled 8-inch pie pan. Cool.

CEREAL PIE CRUST

1½ cups fine crumbs made from any breakfast cereal to which you are not allergic
½ cup melted milk-free margarine
¼ cup sugar (to be used only if unsweetened cereal is used)

Mix all ingredients together. Line pie pan with mixture by pressing it firmly into place. Chill in refrigerator for 20 minutes. Then fill with any desired filling.

BARLEY FLOUR PIE CRUST 🌀

1½ cups barley flour
1 teaspoon baking powder (egg-free)
½ teaspoon salt
4 tablespoons milk-free margarine
6 tablespoons fruit juice

Preheat oven to 400 degrees. Sift dry ingredients together. Cut in milk-free margarine. Add fruit juice and mix to a stiff dough. Line work surface with waxed paper and dust paper with barley flour. Roll out dough on the waxed paper, then transfer to 9-inch pie shell by lifting paper and fitting dough into shell. Remove paper, trim crust, and prick bottom with fork in several places. Bake for 12 to 14 minutes.

UNBAKED GRAHAM-CRACKER CRUST 🌀

1¼ cups graham-cracker crumbs
¼ cup melted milk-free margarine
1 tablespoon sugar
½ teaspoon cinnamon (optional)

Combine crumbs, melted margarine, sugar and cinnamon and press into bottom of 8-inch pie pan.

BAKED GRAHAM-CRACKER PIE CRUST 🌀

Make the pie shell above and bake 8 minutes, or until golden brown, at 375 degrees. Cool before filling.

PEACH COBBLER ⌐∅♉⌐

 1 cup sugar
 1 tablespoon cornstarch
 2 cups fresh or canned peaches, (reserve liquid)
 ½ cup milk-free margarine

In a saucepan, mix sugar and cornstarch; gradually stir in peaches. Bring to a boil and boil for 1 minute, stirring constantly. Melt ½ cup milk-free margarine in a 2-quart oven proof casserole.

BATTER
 1½ cups sugar
 1 cup flour
 ¼ teaspoon salt
 1½ teaspoons baking powder (egg-free)
 ¾ cup peach juice (add water to make ¾ cup if necessary)

Preheat oven to 350 degrees. Mix 1 cup sugar, flour, salt, and baking powder. Beat in peach juice (that you have drained from the canned peaches) until lumps are gone. Pour batter into the melted margarine. Do not stir. Spoon the peach mixture over the top of the batter. Do not stir. Sprinkle ½ cup sugar over top and bake for 45 minutes, or until top is brown. May be served with nondairy topping.

Note: Cherries or blueberries (canned, fresh or frozen) may be used.

APPLE DUMPLINGS ⌐∅♉⌐

FILLING
 6 medium cooking apples
 ¾ cup sugar
 1 tablespoon cinnamon

CRUST

    2 cups flour
    1 teaspoon salt
    ⅔ cup plus 2 tablespoons shortening
    ½ cup cold water

SAUCE

    1 cup sugar
    ¼ cup cornstarch
    ¼ teaspoon salt
    2 cups water
    1 teaspoon lemon extract or ¼ teaspoon nutmeg

Pare and slice apples; mix sugar and cinnamon into them. Sift flour and salt together and cut shortening in until fine. Add water to make soft dough. Roll half the dough as for pie crust and cut into quarters. Place a spoonful of apples on each, gather the crust and press it together at the top. Repeat with remaining dough. Bake in shallow pan at 375 degrees until brown, about 30 to 40 minutes. Serve warm or cold with sauce.

For sauce, combine dry ingredients and small amount of liquid and stir smooth. Add remaining water and cook over medium heat until it starts to thicken, stirring constantly. Reduce heat and cook until clear; stir in flavoring. Serve warm or cold.

DESSERT SAUCES

STRAWBERRY BUTTER

½ cup soft milk-free margarine
1 10-ounce package frozen strawberries, thawed
⅓ cup powdered sugar

Whip margarine until creamy; drain juice from thawed strawberries. Gradually add berries to margarine, beating well after each addition. Beat in sugar. Chill. Serve with waffles or other hot breads. *Makes 1½ cups strawberry butter.*

ORANGE SAUCE

3 tablespoons sugar
2 tablespoons cornstarch
¼ teaspoon salt
1 teaspoon grated orange peel
1 cup boiling water
2 tablespoons shortening
2 tablespoons orange juice

In a medium saucepan, mix together the sugar, cornstarch, salt and orange peel. Slowly stir in the boiling water, cook, stirring constantly for 5 minutes. Stir in the shortening and orange juice.

LEMON SAUCE ⊘⊟✷

½ cup sugar
2 tablespoons cornstarch
1 cup water
⅛ teaspoon salt
1 teaspoon lemon rind
4 tablespoons lemon juice
2 tablespoons milk-free margarine

Mix sugar and cornstarch with ¼ cup water, add remaining water. Bring to boil and remove from heat. Add remaining ingredients. Cool slightly. Serve over warm cake.

CHOCOLATE SYRUP ⊘⊟✷

½ cup unsweetened powdered cocoa
1 cup water
2 cups sugar
⅛ teaspoon salt
¼ teaspoon vanilla

Mix cocoa and water in saucepan, stir to dissolve cocoa, heat to blend the cocoa and water. Add sugar, stirring to dissolve sugar. Boil for 3 minutes. Add salt and vanilla. Pour into clean pint jar. Store covered in refrigerator. Will keep for several months.
Makes 1 pint

MOCHA SAUCE ⊖🛢✿

>   2 teaspoons unsweetened powdered cocoa
>   1 cup confectioners' sugar
>   ⅓ cup milk-free margarine
>   2 tablespoons strong coffee

Add cocoa to sugar. Cream margarine and add sugar to the margarine gradually while beating until the mixture is fluffy. Add coffee gradually while beating to keep sauce from separating.

Other Desserts

PUDDINGS

APPLE CRISP I $\theta\text{⊞}$✳

　　4 cups sliced cooking apples
　　1 tablespoon lemon juice
　　1 cup quick-cooking or old-fashioned oats, uncooked
　　½ cup brown sugar, firmly packed
　　1 teaspoon cinnamon
　　¼ cup melted milk-free margarine

　　Preheat oven to 375 degrees. Place apples in shallow baking dish. Sprinkle with lemon juice. Combine remaining ingredients; mix until crumbly. Sprinkle crumb mixture over apples. Bake for 30 minutes or until apples are tender.

CHERRY CRISP

　　Substitute canned cherries (not cherry pie filling) for apples in the recipe above.

APPLE CRISP II $\theta\text{⊞}$

　　4 cups apples, peeled and sliced
　　¼ cup water
　　¾ cup flour
　　1 cup sugar
　　1 teaspoon cinnamon
　　½ teaspoon salt
　　½ cup milk-free margarine

Preheat oven to 350 degrees. Place apples and water in a 10 ×
6-inch baking pan. Sift flour, sugar, cinnamon and salt into a bowl.
Cut in margarine until the mixture resembles coarse crumbs. Sprinkle
over the apples. Bake for 40 minutes, or until apples are tender.
Makes 6 servings.

CURRIED FRUIT BAKE

½ cup milk-free margarine
1 cup brown sugar, firmly packed
4 teaspoons curry powder
½ cup chopped nuts
1 No. 2 can pear halves, drained
1 No. 2 can peach halves, drained
1 can pineapple chunks, drained
2 cups plums or prunes
Maraschino cherries

Preheat oven to 350 degrees. Melt margarine; add sugar, curry
powder and nuts. Dry fruit. Alternate layers of fruit in flat casserole,
ending with cherries. Spoon margarine mixture over top of fruit.
Bake for 45 to 60 minutes. Serve while warm.

APPLE-TAPIOCA DESSERT

3 large cooking apples, peeled, cored and sliced
2 cups water
1 cup brown sugar, firmly packed
½ cup quick-cooking tapioca
2 tablespoons lemon juice
½ teaspoon salt
¼ teaspoon nutmeg

Preheat oven to 375 degrees. In a 2-quart casserole arrange apple
slices; set aside. In a 2-quart saucepan combine water, brown sugar,

tapioca, lemon juice and salt; let stand for 5 minutes. Cook over medium heat, stirring constantly, until mixture comes to a full boil. Pour over apples in casserole; sprinkle with nutmeg. Cover and bake for 25 minutes or until apples are tender.

BAKED RICE-AND-PINEAPPLE PUDDING

1 20-ounce can sliced pineapple in its own juice
2½ cups water
1 cup regular long-grain rice, uncooked
½ teaspoon salt
½ teaspoon grated lemon peel
½ cup light brown sugar, firmly packed
2 tablespoons milk-free margarine

Preheat oven to 350 degrees. Into a 2-quart saucepan drain juice from pineapple; add water. Over medium heat, heat juice mixture to boiling. Meanwhile, in a 10 × 6-inch baking dish, combine rice, salt and grated lemon peel. Arrange pineapple slices on top. Pour boiling juice mixture over pineapple. Sprinkle with brown sugar, then dot with margarine. Cover with foil and bake for 30 minutes. Remove foil; bake 30 minutes longer or until rice is tender.

RHUBARB CRUMBLY PUDDING

1½ cups sifted flour
Salt
¼ teaspoon cinnamon
1½ cups sugar
⅓ cup milk-free margarine
4 cups fresh rhubarb, cut into 1-inch pieces
1 tablespoon lemon juice

Preheat oven to 375 degrees. Sift flour with ½ teaspoon salt, cinnamon and ½ cup sugar; cut in margarine. Sprinkle half of mixture into an 8-inch square pan; press down. Mix rhubarb with lemon juice, remaining sugar and ⅛ teaspoon salt; spread over mixture in pan. Sprinkle remaining crumb mixture on top. Bake for 45 to 50 minutes.

Note: Peaches or apples may be used. If so, use ½ teaspoon cinnamon.

APRICOT RICE PUDDING

⅔ cup packaged precooked rice
¼ teaspoon salt
2 tablespoons lemon juice
1 1-pound can peeled apricots, pitted, then quartered
Cinnamon
1 tablespoon milk-free margarine

Preheat oven to 350 degrees. In a 1-quart casserole, combine the rice, salt, lemon juice and apricot pieces and syrup. Sprinkle with cinnamon; dot with milk-free margarine. Bake 20 to 25 minutes. Serve warm.

DANISH FRUIT PUDDING

2 10-ounce packages frozen raspberries, thawed
Dash cinnamon
Finely grated peel of ½ lemon
Juice of ½ lemon
2 tablespoons cornstarch
½ teaspoon vanilla
Generous dash of salt
Slivered almonds

Drain syrup from the raspberries into medium saucepan. Mix in cinnamon, peel, juice, cornstarch, vanilla and salt to form smooth paste; stir into raspberry syrup. Cook, stirring constantly, until thickened and smooth. Stir in raspberries; refrigerate. When ready to serve, top with almonds.

Makes 4 to 6 servings.

PEACH DELIGHT

1 1-pound 4-ounce can sliced peaches
¼ teaspoon salt
Generous dash nutmeg
⅛ teaspoon cinnamon
2 tablespoons lemon juice
¼ cup quick-cooking tapioca
1 cup boiling water

Preheat oven to 375 degrees. In a 1½-quart casserole, mix the peaches, salt, nutmeg, cinnamon, lemon juice, tapioca; stir in the boiling water. Bake 30 minutes, or until tapioca is clear. (Stir occasionally.) Serve warm or cold.

Makes 6 servings.

CHERRY DELIGHT

1 1-pound can pitted red sour cherries
¼ teaspoon salt
Generous dash of nutmeg
1 tablespoon lemon juice
⅓ cup quick-cooking tapioca
¾ cup boiling water

Prepare as directed for Peach Delight (above).

BAKED APPLE SURPRISE

2 medium bananas, mashed
1 tablespoon lemon juice
1/4 cup sugar
Dash of salt
1/4 teaspoon nutmeg
6 medium baking apples
1 cup orange juice or pineapple juice

Preheat oven to 375 degrees. Mix the mashed bananas, lemon juice, sugar, salt and nutmeg. Wash and core apples; place in a large baking dish. Fill apples with banana mixture; pour the orange juice or pineapple juice over apples. Bake for 1 hour or until tender, basting occasionally with the juice. Cool and serve warm, or chill and serve cold; top with orange sauce.

APPLE TAPIOCA

1/3 cup tapioca
1 cup brown sugar, firmly packed
4 cups sliced tart apples
2 cups water
2 tablespoons lemon juice
2 tablespoons milk-free margarine
1/2 teaspoon cinnamon
1/2 teaspoon salt

Mix all of the above ingredients and let stand for 5 minutes. Bring to a boil, stirring often. Simmer until apples are tender, about 12 minutes. Serve warm with a sprinkle of nutmeg and some non-dairy topping if desired.

BANANA-ORANGE TAPIOCA ⎡🌿🍯🌼⎤

 ½ cup sugar
 3 tablespoons quick-cooking tapioca
 ¼ teaspoon salt
 2 cups orange juice
 1 tablespoon lemon juice
 ½ teaspoon grated lemon rind
1 or 2 bananas, sliced or diced

Combine sugar, tapioca and salt in saucepan; add orange juice. Let stand 5 minutes. Cook and stir over medium heat until mixture comes to a boil. Remove from heat and stir in lemon juice and rind. Cool, stirring once after 20 minutes. Chill. Top with bananas or stir them in.

Makes 6 servings.

FRUIT-JUICE TAPIOCA ⎡🌿🍯🌼⎤

 ¼ cup quick-cooking tapioca
2½ cups pineapple juice or 2¼ cups apple juice
 ¾ cup sugar
Dash of salt

Mix all ingredients in a saucepan and let stand for 5 minutes. Cook and stir over medium heat until mixture comes to a boil. Cool for 20 minutes. Then stir well and spoon into dessert dishes. Chill.

APPLESAUCE CRISP (PUDDING) ⌷

    1 cup rolled oats, uncooked
    ½ cup sifted flour
    ¼ teaspoon salt
    1 cup light brown sugar, firmly packed
    1 teaspoon cinnamon
    ⅓ cup milk-free margarine
    1½ cups applesauce

Mix together rolled oats, flour, salt, brown sugar, and cinnamon; add margarine and mix until crumbly. Place half of the mixture in a greased 8-inch square pan. Cover with applesauce and sprinkle with remaining crumb mixture. Bake 40 to 45 minutes at 350 degrees.

CANDY

COCONUT PENUCHE ⌷

    2 cups brown sugar, firmly packed
    1 cup granulated sugar
    ½ teaspoon salt
    1½ cups nondairy creamer
    ¼ cup milk-free margarine
    2 teaspoons vanilla
    1½ cups flaked coconut

Combine sugars, salt and creamer. Cook, stirring constantly, until sugar dissolves and mixture boils. Continue cooking until a small amount of mixture forms a soft ball in cold water (or to a temperature of 240 degrees), stirring frequently after mixture begins to thicken. Remove from heat. Add margarine and vanilla. Cool until lukewarm without stirring. Add coconut. Then beat until mixture loses its gloss. Turn at once into lightly greased 8 × 8 × 2-inch pan. Cool, then cut into squares.

Makes 36 large pieces.

Note: For nut penuche, add ¾ cup broken pecans or walnuts instead of coconut.

OLD-FASHIONED MOLASSES-COCONUT BALLS

⅔ cup sugar
⅓ cup light molasses
3 tablespoons light corn syrup
3 tablespoons hot water
1 tablespoon milk-free margarine
2 teaspoons vinegar
⅛ teaspoon salt
2⅔ cups flaked coconut

In a saucepan, combine all ingredients except the coconut. Place over medium heat and cook, stirring occasionally, until a small amount of mixture forms a slightly firm ball in cold water (or to a temperature of 240 degrees). Remove from heat. Cool about 10 minutes. Stir in coconut. Beat until mixture becomes creamy and forms a soft mass, about 1 minute. Roll pieces of the mixture, with greased (use milk-free margarine) fingers or palms, into balls about 2 inches in diameter, or smaller ¾-inch balls. Place candies on waxed paper and cool until firm. Store in tightly covered container in a cool place.

Makes 16 large or 5½ dozen small balls.

BUTTERSCOTCH PUDDING FUDGE ⌐θ♯♦⌐

1 package butterscotch pudding and pie-filling mix
½ cup granulated sugar
½ cup brown sugar, firmly packed
⅓ cup liquid nondairy creamer
2 tablespoons milk-free margarine

Combine pudding mix, sugars and creamer in a saucepan. Mix well. Cook and stir over low heat until sugar is completely dissolved. Continue to cook until mixture comes to a full boil. Boil 2 minutes. Remove from heat, add margarine and beat at once until mixture is thickened and loses its gloss. Turn into a greased 9 × 4-inch loaf pan. Chill. Cut into 1-inch squares.
Makes 36.

Note: If desired, ½ cup broken nuts or flaked coconut may be added when the mixture has thickened.

COCONUT ORANGE PEEL ⌐θ♯♦⌐

2 large oranges
Cold water
Sugar (about 2 cups)
2 to 3 cups flaked coconut

Wash oranges and remove peel in quarters. If white inner skin is excessive, scrape off part of it. Cut peel into ¼-inch strips. Place in a saucepan and cover with cold water. Bring to a boil, then drain off water. Repeat 2 more times, covering with water, boiling and draining. Measure or weigh the peel. Combine in saucepan with an equal amount of sugar. Cover with water. Bring to a boil and cook until syrup is almost absorbed. Remove from heat and place peel on racks to drain for 1 minute. Roll quickly in coconut, then return to racks to cool.
Makes 1 pound candied peel.

CHOCOLATE FUDGE ⊖ 🏠 ♣

    2 cups sugar
    2 tablespoons cocoa
    ½ cup corn syrup
    ¼ cup liquid nondairy creamer
    ¼ cup water
    2 tablespoons milk-free margarine
    1 teaspoon vanilla
    ½ cup chopped nuts (optional)

Mix sugar, cocoa, and corn syrup in a large saucepan. Add creamer and water (well mixed) to the sugar mixture. Cook until mixture forms soft ball in cold water or registers 240 degrees on a candy thermometer. Remove from heat. Add margarine and vanilla and beat until candy starts to turn dull. Add nuts. Pour into greased dish. Cut when firm.

NO-CHOCOLATE CHOCOLATE FUDGE ⊖ 🏠 ♣

    2 cups sugar
    ¾ cup nondairy liquid creamer
    ¼ cup carob powder
    ¼ cup coffee
    3 tablespoons milk-free margarine
    1 teaspoon vanilla
    ½ cup chopped nuts (optional)

Combine the first 5 ingredients in a saucepan. Bring to a boil. Stir until mixture is smooth. Boil to 240 degrees on a candy thermometer, or until mixture forms a soft ball in cold water. Remove from fire and beat with a wooden spoon until thick and creamy. Stir in vanilla and nuts. Pour into greased 8 × 8-inch pan. Cool until hard. Cut into squares.
Makes 25.

MARSHMALLOW FUDGE *⊖⊕✳*

> 4 cups miniature marshmallows (or 32 large marshmallows)
> ⅔ cup liquid nondairy creamer
> ¼ cup milk-free margarine
> 1½ cups sugar
> ¼ teaspoon salt
> 1 large package (12 ounces) chocolate chips
> 1 teaspoon vanilla
> ½ cup chopped nuts

Combine marshmallows, liquid nondairy creamer, margarine, sugar and salt in a saucepan. Cook and stir until mixture comes to a full boil. Then boil for 5 minutes over medium heat, stirring constantly. Remove from heat and add chocolate chips. Beat until chips are melted. Add vanilla and nuts and beat until blended. Pour into greased 9 × 9 × 2-inch pan. Chill.

Makes 2½ pounds.

PEANUT-BUTTER FUDGE *⊖⊕✳*

> 2 cups sugar
> ¾ cup water
> ½ cup peanut butter
> 1 teaspoon vanilla
> Chocolate chips (semisweet) or shredded coconut (optional)

Stir the sugar and water together and boil to the soft-ball stage, 240 degrees on a candy thermometer. Remove from heat and add the peanut butter and vanilla. Beat thoroughly. Semisweet chips or coconut may be added. Pour quickly, or drop immediately by teaspoonfuls onto waxed paper.

8-MINUTE CHOCOLATE FUDGE \[⊖♆♦\]

 2 cups sugar
 2 squares unsweetened chocolate
Dash salt
¼ cup water
¼ cup nondairy creamer
 2 tablespoons milk-free margarine
 1 teaspoon vanilla
½ cup chopped walnuts (optional)

Combine sugar, chocolate, salt, water and creamer in saucepan and place over high heat. Bring to boil; lower to medium heat. Boil, stirring occasionally, until ingredients are blended. This should take 4 minutes at the most; color will look more even. Remove from heat; immediately add margarine and vanilla. Beat with mixer until batter starts to thicken; quickly add nuts and pour into shallow, greased 5 × 9-inch pan. Cool.

CHOCOLATE ALMOND TOFFEE \[⊖♆♦\]

 1 cup brown sugar, firmly packed
 1 cup granulated sugar
⅓ cup white corn syrup
½ cup water
⅛ teaspoon salt
⅓ cup milk-free margarine
 1 6-ounce package semisweet chocolate, melted
½ cup chopped toasted almonds

Combine sugars, syrup, water, and salt in heavy saucepan. Blend thoroughly. Place over medium heat. Stir until sugar is dissolved and mixture is boiling moderately. Cook to firm-ball stage, 245 degrees. Add margarine and continue cooking to hard-crack stage, 290 degrees. Pour into lightly oiled 9 × 9-inch pan. Cool until hard and brittle. Spread with half the melted chocolate and top with half the chopped almonds. Loosen and do the same to other side and break into various-sized pieces.

BUTTER CRUNCH

 1 cup milk-free margarine
 1 cup sugar
 2 tablespoons water
 1 tablespoon light corn syrup
 ¾ cup finely chopped nuts
 4 ounces semisweet chocolate

Melt the margarine in a 2-quart saucepan over low heat. Remove from heat, add the sugar. With a wooden spoon, stir the mixture until it is well blended. Return to low heat, stir rapidly until thoroughly mixed and begins to bubble. Add the water and corn syrup, mix well. Keep heat low, stirring frequently; cook until candy thermometer registers 290 degrees (brittle stage, 15 to 20 minutes). Remove from heat at once. Sprinkle nuts over surface and quickly mix in. Pour out on lightly greased cookie sheet. With spatula, spread ¼ inch thick. Cool to room temperature. Partially melt 2 ounces chocolate over boiling water. Remove from water, stir until melted. Spread evenly over crunch. Set aside until firm, then turn over, melt the rest of the chocolate and spread other side. When firm, break in pieces. Store in tightly covered container in a cool place.

PEANUT BRITTLE 🎉

    2 cups sugar
    ½ cup water
    1 cup light corn syrup
    2 cups raw peanuts
Dash of salt
    1 heaping teaspoon egg-free baking soda
    1 teaspoon vanilla

Combine sugar, water and syrup in large heavy saucepan and boil to the hard-ball stage. Check either by the cold-water method or use a candy thermometer. Remove from heat. Add raw peanuts and salt. Mixture will be quite thick. Return to fire and boil until golden brown and the nuts smell done. Take from the fire. Add baking soda and vanilla. Pour out on a buttered pan. When thoroughly cooled, crack into pieces and serve.

ICE CREAMS AND ICES

STRAWBERRY FROZEN DESSERT 🎉

In a large bowl with fork, break one 16-ounce container frozen nondairy creamer into very small pieces. With mixer at high speed, beat partially frozen creamer until thickened. Reduce speed to low; add ½ cup strawberry preserves and beat until mixed. Pour mixture into 8 × 8-inch baking pan; freeze about 1¼ hours. In chilled large bowl with mixer at low speed, beat mixture until smooth. Return to pan; cover and freeze.

Makes about 6 servings.

TROPICAL FROZEN DESSERT

3 cups sugar
3 cups water
Juice of 3 oranges
Juice of 3 lemons
3 bananas
7-Up

Bring water and sugar to a boil for 5 minutes, cool and add the juice of the oranges and lemons and the bananas, mashed with a fork. Pour into trays and freeze. When ready to serve, break into pieces with a fork and place in individual sherbet dishes and fill with 7-Up. This is also good as a fruit cocktail if used when slushy.

FROZEN FRUIT CUBES

1 cup sugar
1 cup water
1 banana
2 tablespoons lemon juice
1 cup orange juice
1 No. 2 can crushed pineapple (2 cups)

Dissolve sugar in water, mash the banana, add lemon juice, orange juice, pineapple and sugar-water mixture. Freeze in two ice-cube trays, store in freezer containers.
Makes 28 frozen cubes suitable for dessert or appetizer.

LEMON ICE

2½ cups sugar
¼ teaspoon salt
3 cups water
3 teaspoons grated lemon rind (3 lemons)
1 cup lemon juice (5½ lemons)

Place sugar, salt and water over low hat, stir until sugar is dissolved. Boil 5 minutes, cool, add lemon rind and juice, pour into freezer tray and freeze until mushy. Scrape into a well-chilled bowl, beat with chilled beater until smooth, but do not allow ice to melt. Return promptly to freezer tray, beat 2 to 3 times during freezing. Freeze firm, serve in dishes which have been chilled.

BANANA SHERBET

1 tablespoon gelatin
3 cups water
2 cups sugar
Juice of 4 lemons
4 oranges, cut into small wedges
2 ripe bananas, mashed

Soak gelatin 5 minutes in 1 cup water, heat rest of water with sugar to make syrup. Dissolve gelatin mixture in syrup, cool. When cool, add fruits, place in ice-cube tray and freeze.

CRANBERRY SHERBET

1 cup sugar
1 cup water
2 cups cranberries
½ cup grapefruit juice

Cook first 3 ingredients 15 minutes, cool. Pour into electric blender, blend 1 minute, add grapefruit juice and blend ½ minute more. Pour into refrigerator tray and freeze.

PINEAPPLE SHERBET

2 cups grated fresh pineapple
2 cups canned unsweetened pineapple juice
1 teaspoon finely grated lemon rind
2 cups water
2 cups sugar

Mix together all the ingredients in a saucepan. Boil for 5 minutes. Strain. Cool. Pour mix into desired refrigerator ice tray or mold, and freeze without stirring in freezing compartment. Serve.

CANTALOUPE SHERBET

3 cups water
1½ cups sugar
4 cups fresh cantaloupe pulp (about 2 medium-size melons, 2¼ pounds each)
2 tablespoons fresh lemon juice

Combine water and sugar in a saucepan. Boil for 5 minutes. Cool. Remove cantaloupe from shell and purée in an electric blender on high speed. Add the cantaloupe pulp and lemon juice to syrup. Pour into desired refrigerator tray or mold, and freeze without stirring in freezing compartment of refrigerator. During freezing process, remove from freezer and beat. Return to freezer. Serve.

Makes ½ gallon.

CHERRY SHERBET

4 cups water
1¾ cups sugar
2 cups fresh or canned cherry juice
⅛ teaspoon salt
1 tablespoon fresh lemon juice

In a saucepan, combine water and sugar. Boil for 5 minutes. Cool. Mix together sugar syrup, cherry juice, salt and lemon juice. (Fresh cherry juice may be obtained by puréeing fresh cherries in a blender, or by pressing cherries through a sieve and then straining through cheesecloth.)

Pour into desired refrigerator ice tray or mold, and freeze without stirring in freezing compartment of refrigerator. During freezing process, remove from freezer and beat. Return to freezer. Serve.

Makes 1½ gallons.

APRICOT SHERBET

4 cups water
1 cup sugar
2½ cups canned apricot nectar
2 tablespoons lemon juice

Combine water and sugar in a saucepan. Boil for 5 minutes. Cool.

Add apricot nectar and lemon juice to sugar syrup.

Pour into desired refrigerator ice tray or mold and freeze without stirring in freezing compartment of refrigerator.

During freezing process, remove from freezer and beat. Return to freezer. Serve.

Makes ½ gallon.

ORANGE VELVET SHERBET

    1 quart Coffee Rich
    ½ cup lemon juice
    3½ cups orange juice (1 6-ounce can frozen orange juice
        reconstituted)
    3 cups sugar
    1 tablespoon unflavored gelatin
    ¼ cup cold water

Blend together Coffee Rich, citrus juices, and sugar until sugar is dissolved. Dissolve gelatin in cold water; melt over hot water bath. Beating, add to Coffee Rich mixture until well blended. Freeze until firm using 8 parts ice to 1 part salt, or in ice trays in the freezer.

ORANGE SHERBET

    1½ cups sugar
    ½ cup light corn syrup
    3 cups water
    ¼ teaspoon salt
    ½ cup fresh lemon juice
    2 cups fresh orange juice

Mix together sugar, corn syrup, water and salt in a saucepan. Cook, stirring, on low heat for 5 minutes. Cool. Add lemon juice and orange juice to the cooled mixture. Pour mixture into desired refrigerator ice tray or mold, and freeze without stirring in freezing compartment. Serve.

BLACKBERRY SHERBET $\boxed{\theta \, \text{❀} \, ✤}$

4 cups water
1 cup sugar
3 cups fresh blackberry purée (about 1 full quart blackberries)
2 tablespoons fresh lemon juice

Combine water and sugar in saucepan. Boil 5 minutes. Cool.

Add blackberry purée and lemon juice to sugar syrup. (To purée blackberries, use an electric blender on medium speed.)

Pour into desired refrigerator ice tray or mold, and freeze without stirring in freezing compartment of refrigerator.

During freezing process, remove from freezer and beat. Return to freezer. Serve.

Makes ½ gallon.

STRAWBERRY ICE $\boxed{\theta \, \text{❀} \, ✤}$

2 pints strawberries, hulled and sliced
1 cup sugar
¾ cup fresh lime juice
½ cup fresh orange juice
1¼ cups water

Combine berries, sugar, lime and orange juices and let stand for about 2 hours, stirring occasionally. Stir in water. Purée in two batches, using a blender. Strain through a fine sieve to remove seeds. Stir purée and pour into metal 8 or 9-inch square pans; freeze.

When mixture has frozen around the edges (about 45 minutes to 1 hour), scrape into a bowl and beat with a whisk to break up crystals. Do not allow mixture to liquefy. Return to pans and freeze again until almost set. Beat again. Freeze until solid, about 1 to 2 hours. Then beat with an electric mixer until fluffy and snowy. Scoop into quart container, cover tightly and freeze until serving time, preferably at least 6 hours.

Makes about 1½ quarts.

WATERMELON ICE ⟨symbols⟩

2 cups water
1¼ cups sugar
4 cups peeled, diced, and deseeded watermelon
1 6-ounce can concentrated pink lemonade
1 cup peeled, diced, and deseeded watermelon for garnish (option)

Combine water and sugar in a saucepan. Bring to boil and boil for 5 minutes. Cool. Press watermelon through a sieve or purée in a blender. Add sugar syrup and pink lemonade to puréed watermelon. Freeze.

Makes 1½ quarts.

Note: Cantaloupe Ice can be made by substituting cantaloupe for watermelon, and substituting concentrated orange juice for pink lemonade.

CHERRY WATER ICE ⟨symbols⟩

1 quart water
2¾ cups sugar
1½ cups cherry juice

Bring water and sugar to a boil. Cool. Add cherry juice and freeze. If sweetened cherry juice is used, reduce sugar to 2 cups. Freeze.

Makes 2 quarts.

Note: Grape juice can be substituted for cherry juice to make grape ice.

PHILADELPHIA ICE CREAM ⊖⊞✦

   1 quart Coffee Rich
   ¾ cup sugar
   1 teaspoon vanilla
   1 pinch salt

Mix all ingredients to dissolve sugar. Freeze until firm using 8 parts ice to 1 part salt.

Note: For Coffee Ice Cream, dissolve 1½ tablespoons instant coffee in 2 tablespoons hot water and add to ice-cream mixture. For Maple Nut Ice Cream, add 1 cup finely chopped nuts and substitute maple flavoring for vanilla in ice-cream mix. For Peppermint Ice Cream, substitute ½ pound crushed peppermint stick candy for sugar and vanilla.

BUTTERSCOTCH SWIRL ICE CREAM ⊖⊞✦

   ¼ cup brown sugar
   2 tablespoons milk-free margarine
   2 tablespoons dark corn syrup
   3 tablespoons nondairy creamer

Combine all ingredients; boil 2 minutes. Cool. Fold into 1 pint vanilla ice cream for marbled effect. Freeze.

APRICOT WATER ICE ☐

2¼ cups sugar
1 quart water
1½ to 1¾ cups fresh, canned, or frozen apricots

Bring the sugar and water to a fast boil. If canned apricots are used, reduce the sugar to 1½ cups. Crush apricots to a pulp and strain; add to water. Cool and freeze.
Makes 2 quarts.

ICE-CREAM SANDWICHES ☐

Any flavor ices
Graham crackers

Place some of the ice between two halves of a graham cracker. Smooth edges and wrap in foil paper. Place in the freezer. After they freeze the graham cracker becomes soft and won't break when you bite into it.

Snacks
& Beverages

SNACKS

PEANUT BAKED SNACK MIX

¼ cup milk-free margarine
2 tablespoons peanut butter
¼ teaspoon cinnamon
2 cups bite-size shredded wheat cereal
2 cups oat cereal
½ cup shelled peanuts

Preheat oven to 350 degrees. In a small saucepan melt the milk-free margarine, peanut butter and cinnamon. Combine the shredded wheat, oat cereal and peanuts in a 13 × 9-inch baking pan. Pour on margarine mixture and toss. Bake 10 to 12 minutes or until crisp.

HOMEMADE GRANOLA

4 cups oatmeal (not quick-cooking)
½ cup wheat germ
½ cup corn oil
½ cup honey or brown sugar
2 teaspoons vanilla
1 cup sunflower seeds
¾ cup chopped nuts
¾ cup dates and/or raisins

Combine oatmeal and wheat germ in a large bowl. Mix together oil, honey or brown sugar, and vanilla. Drizzle over cereals and mix well; spread on greased baking sheet. Bake at 225 degrees for 45 minutes. Stir in remaining ingredients; bake 15 minutes longer.

Note: To vary granola to suit your own tastes, change ingredients or amounts. Other dried fruits, bran, sesame seeds, coconut, or almost any grain or seed you have on hand can be used.

OATMEAL BREAD CUT-OUTS

Preheat oven to 250 degrees. Select a cookie cutter no larger than a slice of bread. Using a thin slice of the Oatmeal Bread (page 154) or any other milk-free and egg-free bread, make one cut-out per slice and place on cookie sheet. Bake in oven for 15 minutes until cut-outs are crisp. Meanwhile, over medium heat, heat honey until it is thinner and easier to stir. Remove from heat. With a brush spread each cut-out with honey, then sprinkle with chopped pecans.

OVEN CARAMEL CORN

2 cups brown sugar
½ cup white corn syrup
1 cup milk-free margarine
1 teaspoon salt
1 teaspoon butter flavoring
1 teaspoon burnt sugar flavoring
½ teaspoon baking soda
6 quarts popped corn

Combine brown sugar, syrup, margarine and salt. Boil 5 minutes. Remove from heat, stirring in flavors and soda. Pour immediately over corn that has been put into roaster. Spoon hot syrup through corn. (Be sure that all of the corn is covered.) Place in oven set at 250 degrees. Stir every 15 minutes and cook for 1 hour. Store in tightly sealed container.

PINEAPPLE COCONUT TIDBITS

Cut fresh pineapple into 1-inch squares. Dip first in honey, then in shredded coconut.

NUTTY BANANAS

Mix ½ cup peanut butter with 2 tablespoons of water (add more to get a creamy texture). Peel 2 bananas; cut in half crosswise. Insert a stick in each flat end. Spread banana with peanut-butter mixture and roll in chopped nuts. Place on waxed paper and freeze until firm, about 2 hours.

CRUNCHY CELERY

Fill 4 long ribs of celery with chunky peanut butter, then sprinkle with sunflower seeds (if desired). Cut each rib of celery into about 3-inch-long pieces.

BANANA POPS

Peel bananas and cut in half crosswise; insert ice-cream stick in cut end. Freeze, then dip into maple syrup or honey thinned with warm water. If you are just doing one or two, use brush or spoon. Roll in chopped nuts, cookie crumbs or granola. Return to freezer in covered container.

FROSTY FEAST

Wash and drain seedless grapes and bing cherries, and peel and slice bananas into bite-sized pieces. Arrange on cookie sheet; freeze until solid. Place in covered container and return to freezer. Defrost partially to eat.

FROZEN BANANA SNACK

Cut a banana in half and stick popsicle sticks into the flat ends and place on a piece of waxed paper and freeze. Another way of doing this is to cut the banana into bite-sized pieces and freeze. This tastes like banana ice cream.

BEVERAGES

BANANA FLIP

1 ripe banana, cut up or mashed
¾ cup nondairy creamer
¾ cup ice water
2 teaspoons sugar
2 tablespoons lemon instant pudding

Mash banana if not using blender. Add remaining ingredients. Shake in jar or blend in blender. Let stand a minute before serving.
Makes 2 servings.

CREAMY SHAKE

  ½ cup nondairy creamer
  ½ cup ice water
  1 teaspoon sugar
  ¼ cup mashed strawberries
  1 tablespoon vanilla instant pudding

Shake all ingredients in a jar or blend in blender. Let stand a minute before serving.

Note: In place of the strawberries, try substituting your own flavor of jam.

FRESH FRUIT SMOOTHIE

  1 peach, cut up (optional)
  1 banana, cut up
  1 cup pineapple juice
  1 cup orange juice
  2 cracked ice cubes
  1 tablespoon sugar

Omit peach and mash banana if not using blender. Shake all ingredients in a jar or blend in blender.
  Makes 3 servings.

HOT CHOCOLATE

1½ tablespoons cocoa
4 tablespoons brown sugar
½ teaspoon cornstarch
2 tablespoons nondairy powdered creamer

Stir the first 3 ingredients into 1½ cups of water. Cook over medium heat, beating slowly until mixture comes to a boil. Remove from heat and add nondairy powdered creamer and whip vigorously for a few minutes.

SPARKLING FRUIT JUICE

Fill a glass ¾ full with favorite juice. Add club soda or seltzer to fill glass; add a piece of fruit if desired.

SLUSH

2 bananas, mashed
1 cup sugar
1 can crushed pineapple
1 can concentrated orange juice
Grated rind of 1 orange
Grated rind of 1 lemon
3 tablespoons lemon juice
1 pint ginger ale

Combine above ingredients and freeze. Chop finely when frozen. Refreeze. Serve in small cups.
Makes 12 servings.

BANANA CRUSH ⊘♻♦

4 cups sugar
6 cups water
1 46-ounce can pineapple juice
2 12-ounce cans frozen orange juice concentrate, thawed
1 12-ounce can frozen lemonade concentrate, thawed
6 bananas, mashed
7 28-ounce bottles lemon-lime carbonated beverages, or equal
amounts of lemon juice and ginger ale may be used

Dissolve sugar in water. Add juices and mashed bananas. Put through food mill. Stir well into carbonated beverages.

Makes 60 servings at 6 ounces each.

STRAWBERRY FRUIT CRUSH ⊘♻♦

1 cup fresh or frozen strawberries
Juice of 1 lime
1 banana
Juice of 2 oranges
1 cup cracked ice

Blend strawberries, lime juice, banana and a little orange juice in a blender until smooth. Add the remaining orange juice and cracked ice. Blend again.

Makes 2 cups.

FRUIT COOLER

Pour ¾ cup cold water into blender; add 1 heaping tablespoon of each:

> frozen apple juice concentrate
> orange juice concentrate
> pineapple juice concentrate

Whirl just to blend.

BIRTHDAY PARTY PUNCH

12 bottles of strawberry soda pop
1 large can of pineapple juice

Have all ingredients cold. Mix just before serving.
Makes 25 small servings.

HOT MULLED GRAPE JUICE

1 to 2 cinnamon sticks
4 whole cloves
4 whole allspice
2 quarts grape juice
¼ cup sugar

Tie the spices in a small bag and drop into a large saucepan. Pour in the grape juice and sugar, bring the mixture to a boil. Let stand for 10 minutes. Remove the spice bag.
Makes 8 servings.

HOT SPICED CRANBERRY PUNCH

Tie in cheesecloth bag:
  2 teaspoons nutmeg
  2 teaspoons cinnamon
  2 teaspoons allspice
  1½ cups tea leaves

Steep these in 20 cups hot water for 20 minutes. Remove bag and add:

  6 cups sugar
  4 cups orange juice
  2 cups lemon juice
  1 gallon cranberry juice cocktail
  12 cups hot water

Serve piping hot.
Makes 25 servings.

For Further Reading

Emerling, Carol G., and Eugene D. Jonkers, *The Allergy Cookbook*. New York: Barnes & Noble, 1975.

Frazier, Claude A., *Coping with Food Allergy*. New York: Times Books, 1974.

Little, Billie, *Recipes for Allergies*. New York: Grosset and Dunlap, 1971.

May, Charles d., and S. Allan Bock, "Adverse Reactions to Food Due to Hypersensitivity." In *Allergy: Principle and Practice* (edited by E. Middleton, Jr., C. Reed, E. Ellis), pp. 1159–1171. St. Louis: Mosby, 1978.

Rapp, Doris J., *Allergies and Your Child*. New York: Holt, Rinehart and Winston, 1972.

Index